THE SIMPLE REMOVAL FROM OFFICE

A Historical Synopsis and a Commentary

The Catholic University of America
Canon Law Studies
No. 285

The Simple Removal from Office

A Historical Synopsis and a Commentary

A DISSERTATION

SUBMITTED TO THE FACULTY OF THE SCHOOL OF CANON LAW OF THE CATHOLIC UNIVERSITY OF AMERICA IN PARTIAL FULFILLMENT OF THE REQUIREMENTS FOR THE DEGREE OF DOCTOR OF CANON LAW

BY THE
REV. CHESTER JOSEPH THOMPSON, A.B., J.C.L.
Priest of the Archdiocese of San Francisco

The Catholic University of America Press
Washington, D. C.
1951

NIHIL OBSTAT:

EDWARDUS G. ROELKER, S.T.D., J.C.D.

Censor Deputatus.

Washingtonii, D. C., die 30 maii, 1948.

IMPRIMATUR:

✠ JOANNES J. MITTY, D.D.

Archiepiscopus Sancti Francisci

Sancti Francisci, die 3 iunii, 1948.

MURRAY AND HEISTER
WASHINGTON, D. C.

PRINTED BY
TIMES AND NEWS PUBLISHING CO.
GETTYSBURG, PA., U. S. A.

TO MY FATHER
AND IN
MEMORY OF
MY MOTHER

TABLE OF CONTENTS

TABLE OF CONTENTS (Continued)

TABLE OF CONTENTS (Continued)

TABLE ON CONTENTS (Continued)

FOREWORD

The purpose of this dissertation is to present the principles and application of the law regarding the simple removal from office. In canon 192, § 3, of the Code of Canon Law, the ordinary is given the power to remove from office those incumbents who are removable apart from the use of a legal process. For such a removal the ordinary need have only a just cause according to his prudent judgment, even though there is no offense on the part of the cleric. Nevertheless the ordinary is bound to observe natural equity, although he is not at all bound to follow a definite form of procedure, except in the removal of removable pastors, for which removal the prescriptions of canons 2157-2161 must be followed.

It is, then, with the removal from ecclesiastical offices, other than those of removable pastors whose removal must follow a definite procedure, that this work is concerned. Accordingly it bears the title *The Simple Removal from Office*. For the removal from office may be classified under three types or species: 1) the judicial removal, in which the rules of a strict canonical trial are followed, or at least the rules of a process as outlined in Titles XXX-XXXII of the Fourth Book of the Code, and which, since it is intended as a punishment for grave crimes, is called a privation of office in the strict sense; 2) the economic or administrative removal, which is applied by means of an administrative process, and which is not necessarily intended as a punishment; and, finally 3) the simple removal, which a superior undertakes for a just cause and with all due observance of the demands of natural equity, and which he may apply apart from the use of any formalities with regard to removable incumbents. This latter type is sometimes called an *ad nutum* effected removal from office, or also a revocation of the appointment.

The present work is divided into two parts. The first part, by way of historical synopsis, investigates the evidences and developments in the law regarding the simple removal from office before the time when the present Code became the universal law of the

Church. It also deals with the further application of the legal principles underlying the act of the simple removal from office, as that application became manifest in the post-Tridentine Constitutions of the Popes and in the responses of the Sacred Roman Congregations.

The second part reflects an attempt to present as clearly as possible the proper interpretation of the law regarding the simple removal from office as it exists in the Code of Canon Law. After an introductory chapter, which deals with some necessary preliminary notions and definitions, the work proceeds to a consideration of the competent superior for the act of simple removal, and of the various ecclesiastical incumbents of offices who are subject to this type of removal. Next, stress is laid on the requirements for the legitimate use of this power, namely, the presence of a just cause and the due observance of natural equity. Finally, a few remarks are offered regarding the means of redress available to the cleric who is removed from his office.

The writer wishes to take this occasion to express his sincere gratitude to the Most Reverend John J. Mitty, D.D., Archbishop of San Francisco, for the opportunity to pursue advanced studies in Canon Law; to the Faculty of the School of Canon Law of the Catholic University of America for their profitable instruction and assistance; and to all others who have aided in any way in the completion of this work.

PART ONE

Historical Synopsis

CHAPTER I

The Law Regarding Simple Removal From Office Before the Council of Trent

The present chapter proposes to consider the various offices which before the Council of Trent were subject to the power of the bishop as far as the removal of their incumbents from them was concerned. The consideration will be limited for the most part to those offices which may be regarded as the juridical forebears of the offices whose incumbents are now designated as removable from office. Thus, for example, the office of vicar forane will be traced back to its beginnings in the office of the archpriest. The office of the archdeacon, on the other hand, will be treated not for the reason that it was the exact prototype of the office of vicar general, but in view simply of its closer resemblance than that of other offices to the position later held by the vicar general.

In the historical survey of these offices the problem will be to ascertain what method of removal was open to the ordinary, or to the legitimate superior, and to discover the historical background of the power now granted in canon 192, § 3, of the Code, whereby the ordinary can for a just cause and without any juridical process displace the incumbents from their office.

In general, it may be stated that the answer to the principle which underlies the act of simple removal is to be found in the sharp contrast between those offices which go back to antiquity and those which the Church created in the later Middle Ages in order to meet the demands of administrative needs. In the early centuries the bishop freely designated the offices of his clergy. Both their appointment to and their removal from office depended completely on his will.[1] Permanent offices existed, however, long before the existence of benefices. Yet the stability of offices was greatly increased with the rise of benefices in the ninth century, so

[1] Sipos, *Enchiridion Iuris Canonici* (Pécs: Ex Typographia "Haladás. R. T., 1926), p. 127.

that by the tenth century, at least in the West, all offices in the diocese became connected with a benefice—and that, too, a benefice which was perpetual, both objectively and subjectively, so that the incumbent was not removable at will, i.e., *ad nutum.*[2] On the contrary, appointment to these offices, invested with ordinary and proper powers, so stabilized the position of the incumbent that he could be removed only by means of a trial.

Those offices, on the other hand, which were created with a view to meeting administrative needs, such as that of the vicar general, that of the vicar forane, and those of the various parochial vicars—at least those who were appointed simply for a temporary duration—did not enjoy the same degree of stability. Such offices connoted at most a manual benefice, and were invested with powers of a derived or vicarious character. Their incumbents could be removed in a simple manner without the process of a trial or apart from juridical proceedings.

SECTION I. THE ARCHDEACON; PERMANENCE OF OFFICE

Legislation in the early centuries regarding the removal of the archdeacon, in fact regarding removal from all offices, suffers from ambiguity, so that it is not always possible to determine whether removal, or deprivation, or degradation was meant.[3] Be that as it may, it seems evident from the authors, especially the decretalists, as will be pointed out below, that the archdeacon was not to be removed except by means of a canonical sentence, that is, in a judiciary manner.

Before any consideration is given to the causes for which the archdeacon could be removed, it should be noted that in the ninth century another type of archdeacon was created with some jurisdiction over a determined territory. The non-urban territory of the

[2] Sipos, *op. cit.*, p. 127

[3] Thomassinus (1619-1695) noted that even in the fifth century the bishop could by his sole action appoint the archdeacon, but he could not similarly remove (*exauthorare*) him without cause and without a trial. Cf. *Vetus et Nova Ecclesiae Disciplina* (10 vols., Magontiaci, 1787), Pars I, lib. II, cap. 17, n. 5 (hereinafter this work will be referred to as Thomassinus). But it is not altogether clear from his statement whether removal or deposition was meant.

diocese was divided up into two or more archdeaconries, over each of which presided an archdeacon. These were called rural or minor, and thus became distinguished from the major archdeacon of the cathedral city, who quite generally was constituted as the head of the cathedral chapter of canons. By the eleventh century the jurisdiction of the archdeacons was considered as ordinary jurisdiction. Like the archdeacon of the city, so too the rural archdeacon could not be removed except by means of a canonical sentence.[4]

Article I. Removal of Archdeacon for Crimes and Faults

When the system of benefices had developed between the ninth and the twelfth centuries, the title of irremovability was no longer based on the incardination by which a cleric was attached to a certain church for the service of which he had been ordained. The incumbent of a benefice had a perpetual right to receive its revenues, so that he could not be deprived of the benefice except for certain grave crimes of which he was found guilty during a criminal trial.[5]

It would be outside the scope of this work to go further into the question of removal by way of judicial trial regarding such crimes as received mention in the law as causes for removal. Such a subject belongs properly to the question of deprivation in the strict sense, that is, of the removal from office as a punishment for crime, whether inflicted *ipso iure* or by means of the sentence of a superior.

Were there, especially in the later centuries, any misdeeds or acts of malfeasance other than strict crimes for which the archdeacon could be removed from office? Several councils held during the eleventh and twelfth centuries legislated, for example, that one

---

[4] De Meester, *Juris Canonici et Juris Canonico-Civilis Compendium* (ed. nova, 3 vols. in 4, Brugis, 1921-1928), II, 181 (hereafter cited *Compendium*); Zaplotnik, *De Vicariis Foraneis,* The Catholic University of America Canon Law Studies, n. 47 (Washington, D. C.: The Catholic University of America, 1927), p. 29.

[5] Claeys-Bouuaert, *De Canonica Cleri Saecularis Obedientia* (Lovanii, 1904), p. 288; Wernz, *Ius Decretalium* (6 vols., Vol. II, 3. ed., Prati, 1915), II, n. 535; Connor, *The Administrative Removal of Pastors,* The Catholic University of America Canon Law Studies, n. 104 (Washington, D. C.: The Catholic University of America, 1937), p. 9.

who was designated for the office of archdeacon had to receive the sacred Order of the diaconate within a prescribed time under penalty of being deprived of his office.

Thus the Council of Bourges in 1031 legislated: ". . . ut archidiaconatum nullus habeat, nisi Diaconus efficiatur."[6] This law was confirmed by the Council of Clermont (1095) under Pope Urban II (1088-1099), and by the I General Council of the Lateran (1123) under Pope Calixtus II (1119-1124).[7] Again, the Council of London (1127) ordered the bishops to deprive of their office archdeacons who refused to be ordained deacons.[8] Further legislation on the same question was enacted by the II General Council of the Lateran (1139) under Pope Innocent II (1130-1143) and by the Council of Rheims which was held in the year 1148.[9]

No evidence can be found either in the legislation itself or in the teachings of the authors that the archdeacon could be removed in a simple manner aside from any canonical cause and canonical process or sentence. On the contrary, as noted above, in view of the very nature of the benefice which his office implied—a benefice that was perpetual both objectively and subjectively—it seems imperative to conclude with Wernz (1842-1914) that the archdeacon could be removed by means of a judicial sentence of the bishop only for some malfeasance or crime which the law designated as a cause for removal from his office.[10]

Article II. Removal for Other Causes

Further evidence from the Decretals and the works of the commentators on the Decretals confirms the stability of the position of

---

[6] Council of Bourges (1031), c. 4—Mansi, *Sacrorum Conciliorum Nova et Amplissima Collectio* (53 vols. in 60, Paris-Arnhem-Leipzig, 1901-1927), XIX, 503 (hereafter cited as Mansi).

[7] Council of Clermont (1095), c. 3—Mansi, XX, 817, and found in the *Decretum Gratiani* in c. I, D. LX; I General Council of the Lateran (1123), c. 2—Mansi, XXI, 282, and found in the *Decretum* in c. 2, D. LX.

[8] Council of London (1127), c. 4—Mansi, XXI, 356.

[9] II General Council of the Lateran (1139), c. 10—Mansi, XXI, 528, and found in the *Decretum* in c. 3, D. LX; Council of Rheims (1148), c. 9—Mansi, XXI, 716.

[10] Wernz, *Ius Decretalium,* II, nn. 535, 539.

the archdeacon to the extent that he was not removable in a simple manner, not even for such reasonable causes as mental or physical disability and old age.

Clear and definite was the teaching of Pope Honorius III (1216-1227), namely, that an archdeacon who because of a paralysis had lost the use of his tongue was not to be removed from his office, but rather that a coadjutor was to be given him.[11] Moreover, the Glossator remarked that the same was true if the archdeacon had lost his eyesight.[12] The reason for this teaching, according to the Glossator and the commentators on this and similar Decretals, was based on a letter of Pope Gregory the Great (590-604), written in 601 to a certain Columbus, Bishop of Numidia in Mauretania.[13]

Two other letters of the same Pope were referred to in support of this doctrine. One was written to Anatolius, a deacon of Constantinople. In this letter the Pope stated clearly that a bishop who is sick is not to be deprived of his office, but rather that a coadjutor is to be given him in order that the administration of the office may be carried on.[14] The other letter was written to a certain Candidus in 591. In it the Pontiff warned that afflictions were not to be added to afflictions already present.[15]

According to Reiffenstuel (1642-1703), this regulation applied

---

[11] ". . . Archdiacono autem, quem morbo paralytico laborantem officium linguae asseris amisisse, coadiutor est merito adhibendus."—c. 6, X, *de clerico aegrotante vel debilitato,* III, 6; Potthast, *Regesta Pontificum Romanorum inde ab anno post Christum natum MCXCVIII ad annum MCCCIV* (2 vols., Berolini, 1874-1875), n. 799 (hereafter cited as Potthast).

[12] *Glossa Ordinaria,* ad c. 6, *de clerico aegrotante vel debilitato,* III, 6, s.v. *officium linguae.*

[13] "Satis perversum et contra ecclesiasticam probatur esse censuram, ut frustra pro quorundam voluntatibus quis privetur, quem sua culpa vel facinus ab officiis, quo fungitur, gradu non deicit."—c. 7, D. LVI; Jaffé, *Regesta Pontificum Romanorum ab condita Ecclesia ad annum post Christum natum MCXCVIII* (ed. 2. correctam et auctam auspiciis Gulielmi Wattenbach curaverunt S. Loewenfeld, F. Kaltenbrunner, P. Ewald, 2 vols., Lipsiae, 1885-1888), n. 1854 (hereafter cited Jaffé).

[14] C. 1, C. VII, q. I; Jaffé, n. 1819.

[15] "Cum percussio corporalis imminet, utrum pro purgatione, an pro vindicta contingat, Dei in hoc iudicium ignoratur, et ideo non debet a nobis flagellatis addi afflictio, ne nos culpae (quod absit) offensa respiciat . . ."—c. 2, C. VII, q. I; Jaffé, n. 1161.

to other officials as well, that is, not only to prelates who in rank and in dignity were below the archdeacon, especially to those who exercised the care of souls, but also to others who held some different administration or office.[16] It was from the doctrine of the earlier commentators that there was warranted the explanation which was given by Reiffenstuel. Fagnanus (1598-1678), for example, concluded from the Decretals of Gregory IX (1234) that in the event of mental disability, of an incurable disease, and of old age, those who held a beneficed office were not to be removed from office, but were to be given a coadjutor or a vicar.[17]

Hostiensis (1271) listed the opinion of some who took exception to the retention in office of those clerics who were afflicted with leprosy. Concerning such they had made a distinction between bishops and lower prelates. The bishop was not to be removed; he was to be given a coadjutor. Lesser prelates and clerics lower than a bishop were to be removed, and a successor was to be appointed in their stead. But Hostiensis rejected this opinion.[18] According to him and other commentators, the incumbent remained in office as far as the title to that office was concerned; he was merely to be removed from the actual exercise or administration of the office, and a coadjutor was to be supplied. The authors based their conclusion on the remarks of the Glossator.[19]

Such then was the position of the archdeacon and the incumbents of other offices which were established as perpetual benefices. Every indication points to a rigid adherence to this principle, as far as the archdeacon was concerned, up to and including the thirteenth century, for only then did the office of the vicar general become clearly established in the universal Church.

---

[16] Reiffenstuel, *Jus Canonicum Universum* (5 vols. in 6, Romae, 1831-1835), Lib. III, tit. 6, n. 20 (hereafter cited Reiffenstuel).

[17] Fagnanus, *Commentaria in Quinque Libros Decretalium* (5 vols. in 3, Venetiis, 1709), Lib. III, tit. 6, nn. 2-6 (hereafter cited Fagnanus).

[18] C. 4, X, *de clerico aegrotante vel debilitato,* III, 6; Hostiensis (Henricus de Segusio), *Commentaria in Quinque Decretalium Libros* (5 vols. in 3, Venetiis, 1581), Lib. III, *de clerico aegrotante,* cap. 4, n. 1 (hereafter cited *Commentaria*).

[19] *Glossa Ord.,* ad c. 4, X, *de clerico aegrotante vel debilitato,* III, 6, s.v. *administrationis.*

SECTION II. THE VICAR GENERAL—FROM THE THIRTEENTH CENTURY UNTIL THE COUNCIL OF TRENT

In the twelfth and thirteenth centuries the power and jurisdiction of the archdeacon became so extensive that a need was felt for some other official to handle certain administrative functions in the diocese. The bishops desired an official who would be their true vicar (*vicarius in spiritualibus*) and who at the same time would be dependent upon their will. This led to the institution of the office of the vicar general, who in time took over some of the archdeacon's functions.

The practice of constituting these *vicarii principales* (as the Decretals referred to them), or vicars general, was nearly everywhere in vogue a little after the time of Pope Gregory IX (1227-1241), and the Decretals of Pope Boniface VIII (1294-1303) contain a special title concerning them.[20] However, in the *Liber Sextus* there was little that had any bearing on the subject of this work other than the fact that these vicars were recognized as definitely established at the time of Pope Boniface VIII. It was rather in the Decretals of Clement V (1303-1314) that any clear reference was made to the question of the removal of such officials.[21] One of these Decretals, promulgated by Pope John XXII in 1317, offers the basis for the remarks of the commentators regarding the removal of the vicar general.[22] In fact, the glossator on this decretal remarked that the vicar could be removed *ad nutum* by the bishop.[23]

In commenting on this *Glossa* in the Clementine Decretals, Reif-

[20] *De officio vicarii,* I, 13, in VI°.

[21] It is not the purpose here to settle the problem whether the offices of the vicar general and of the diocesan court official were distinct in the beginning. Wernz maintained that a real distinction was made in the larger dioceses of England, of France, and of Germany between the vicar general, who exercised voluntary jurisdiction and administration, and the *officialis,* who exercised jurisdiction in contentious cases and criminal cases. However, the distinction is not found in the common law, for the terms vicar general and *officialis* are used indiscriminately in the Decretals. Cf. Wernz, *Ius Decretalium,* II, n. 800.

[22] C. 2, *de rescriptis,* I, 2, in Clem.

[23] *Glossa Ord.,* ad c. 2, *de rescriptis,* I, 2, in Clem: ". . . de officiali quem episcopus ad nutum removet."

fenstuel listed Rebuffus (1487-1557), Barbosa (1589-1649), and Pirhing (1606-1679) as having supported the teaching that this text applied to the vicar general.[24] The argumentation relied simply upon the assumption that the vicar general did not hold an office which had both objective and subjective perpetuity. Objectively indeed the office had perpetuity, but the incumbent was appointed to it as a temporary and removable occupant of the office. Stress was laid on the vicarious nature of these more recently established offices, which had originated without existing at the same time as benefices. Thus the office suffered from a lack of permanency for its incumbent. As occupant of the office he became removable at the will of the bishop.

While it was true that in accordance with the law the vicar general acquired jurisdiction, and that, too, an ordinary jurisdicdiction,[25] nevertheless he acquired it solely in consequence of his nomination to the office by the bishop. This nomination the bishop could revoke in full accordance with the *Regula Juris* which stated: "Omnis res per quascunque causas nascitur, per easdem dissolvitur."[26] In fine, the vicar general was not vested with a strict juridical title to his office, and thus his office lacked the mainstay of subjective permanency which those enjoyed whose office was at the same time a benefice, for in the latter supposition the incumbents were vested with the title and claim to a continued and abiding possession of the office.[27]

The means of support for such officials as the vicar general and other removable officials was according to the later decretalists derived from a *manual* benefice, which distinguished it from the true and proper benefice.[28]

---

[24] Reiffenstuel, Lib. I, tit. 28, n. 107.

[25] *Glossa Ord.*, ad c. 2, *de officio vicarii*, I, 13, in VI°, s.v. *officialem.*

[26] C. I, X, *de regulis iuris*, V, 41.

[27] Reiffenstuel, Lib. I, tit. 24, n. 7. Note especially in the place cited: "*Vicarius Generalis non est intitulatus in officio.*"

[28] Reiffenstuel, Lib. I, tit. 28, n. 45: "Vicarii temporales vere et proprie non sunt beneficiarii. Ita communis; . . . Ratio est quia vicarii temporales, et ad nutum amovibiles, nullum habent titulum in Beneficio, neque in eo investiuntur"; Ferraris, *Prompta Bibliotheca Canonica, Iuridica, Moralis, Theologica, necnon Ascetica, Polemica, Rubricistica, Historica* (9 vols., Romae, 1885-1899), s.v. *beneficium,* Art I, nn. 35-36 (hereafter cited Fer-

Removal from the office could be effected by the bishop, and indeed validly, even though he had declared under oath that he would not remove the incumbent. It was acknowledged, of course, that in the absence of a just cause the bishop's non-observance of such an oath made him guilty of perjury. Thus, according to Reiffenstuel, the removal from offices of incumbents who were removable *ad nutum* would be entirely dependent upon the free and absolute will of the bishop, and hence was not necessarily regulated by law.[29] Since such offices implied at the most simply the status of a manual benefice,[30] the one who had the power to remove the incumbent of such a benefice could do so without a cause, as long as he was not motivated by malice or hatred, and as long as the act of removal was free of prejudicial discrimination against persons who had a rightfully vested interest in the case.

On the other hand, Schmalzgrueber (1663-1735) somewhat limited the scope of the apparently absolute or completely discretional power of the superior over manual benefices or offices in the matter regarding the removal of their incumbents. This commentator raised the question whether the revocation of an appointment to a manual benefice could be undertaken by the superior with such a degree of free option that there was postulated neither a cause as expressed in the law nor any other reasonable cause. Some authors, he stated, thought that a revocation of this kind in the absence of every reasonable cause was altogether invalid. He carefully pointed out that a reasonable cause was demanded indeed if the act of removal was to be licit in character, for without such a cause the act was certainly illicit, but, so he felt, just as certainly valid. The most that an incumbent could do was to seek either to hinder a malicious removal or, when unlawfully removed, to have

---

raris): "Insuper beneficia alia sunt manualia, seu ad nutum revocabilia, et alia non manualia, seu titularia, quae in titulum perpetuum conferuntur. Manualia sunt illa, quae ad nutum alterius possunt auferri, ideoque dicuntur manualia, quia in alterius manu et dispositione stat illa relinquere, vel auferre, et haec rigorose loquendo non sunt proprie beneficia, cum de natura beneficii proprie dicti sit, ut institutus in eo perpetuo duret; cap. *Sanctorum*, 2, dist. 70."

[29] Reiffenstuel, Lib. III, tit. 5, n. 45: ". . . ad liberam ipsius (conferentis) et absolutam voluntatem, et non necessario regulatum."

[30] Cf. *supra*, footnote n. 28.

recourse to the higher superior for a nullification of the act of removal whenever the demand of utility for the people persuaded such action to be taken on the part of the superior.[31]

SECTION III. THE RURAL ARCHPRIEST, THE RURAL DEAN, AND THE VICAR FORANE

Just at what time the office of vicar forane became instituted in the Church is very difficult to ascertain. Nevertheless it is evident that from the time of the Carlovingians—or at least from the ninth century onward—the bishops were accustomed to constitute rural vicars, whose office it was to be vigilant over the rural clergy, to safeguard the faith and morals of the laity, to secure the preservation of the temporal goods of the Church, and to inform the bishops concerning everything that pertained to the salvation of the faithful living in the country districts.[32]

While it is true that authors are now divided in their opinion whether the vicar forane or rural dean has an ecclesiastical office in the strict sense, still in its origin his work seems to have been constituted as an office in the strict sense. Hence the question of removal from this office is deserving of some historical analysis, if for no other reason than to contrast, from the viewpoint of the incumbent's removal, the ancient office of the archpriest or the rural dean with the later and present office of the vicar forane, who according to the law of the present Code is certainly removable from office at the will of the bishop.[33]

---

[31] Schmalzgrueber, *Jus Ecclesiasticum Universum* (5 vols. in 12, Romae, 1843-1845), Lib. III, tit. 5, n. 37.

[32] C. 4, X, *de officio archipresbyteri,* I, 24: "Ut singulae plebes archipresbyterum habeant; propter assiduam erga populum Dei curam, singulis plebibus archipresbyteros praeesse volumus, qui non solum imperiti vulgi sollicitudinem gerant, verum etiam eorum presbyterorum, qui per minores titulos habitant, vitam iugi circumspectione custodiant, et qua unusquisque industria divinum opus exerceat, episcopo suo renunciet." The Friedberg edition of the Decretals reports this Decretal as taken from a Constitution of the Emperor Lambert after the Council of Ravenna, in the year 898, at the time of Pope John IX (898-900).

[33] Canon 446, § 2: "Vicarius foraneus ad nutum Episcopi amoveri potest"; Coronata, *Institutiones Iuris Canonici* (5 vols., Vol. I, 2. ed., Taurini: Marietti, 1939), I, 559 (hereafter cited *Institutiones*). Cf. the footnote to this reference: "non tamen arbitrario prorsus modo," which the author bases on canon 192, § 3, of the Code.

Article I. The Rural Archpriest and the Rural Dean

The vicar forane had various types of predecessors through the course of history. Such, for example, were the rural archpriests and the rural deans (*decani*). Most of these offices implied a permanent incumbency, that is, for the lifetime of the incumbent.

From the ninth century onward the rural archpriest with ordinary power supervised the pastoral and spiritual care of the towns of his archipresbyterate; he exercised a certain vigilance over the priests and clergy of the district.[34] As to his removal, the bishop could not remove him *ad nutum*. In order to remove him the bishop had to have not only sufficient reasons but also the advice of the other priests of the district.[35]

It was in the ninth century likewise that the office of rural archpriest underwent a change. Until that time the only type of archpriest was the one who presided over the baptismal churches and had under him several priests who cared for the various filial churches within his parish. In time many of these filial churches had acquired the status of parishes, and their rectors became pastors. Hence the status of the old baptismal churches lost much of its significance. Since these several parish priests were all equal among themselves inasmuch as they enjoyed equal power, they remained without an immediate superior to watch over them. For this office the bishops chose from the pastors of the diocese fitting men who were called rural deans (*decani rurales*) or archpriests.[36]

The office of rural dean was generally of permanent duration for the lifetime of the incumbent. It was joined with some parish or benefice, and therefore the rural dean could not be removed from the office except through a canonical sentence.[37] However, there

---

[34] C. 4, X, *de officio archipresbyteri*, I, 24—cf. *supra*, p. 12, footnote n. 32; De Meester, *Compendium*, II, 238.

[35] II Council of Tours (567), c. 7: "Ut episcopus nec archipresbyterum, sine omnium suorum compresbyterorum et abbatum consilio, de loco suo praesumat eiicere, neque per praemia alium ordinare, nisi facto concilio tam abbatum quam presbyterorum suorum . . ."—Mansi, IX, 794; Zaplotnik, *De Vicariis Foraneis*, p. 17.

[36] De Meester, *op. cit.*, II, 238; Zaplotnik, *De Vicariis Foraneis*, p. 29.

[37] Zaplotnik, *De Vicariis Foraneis*, p. 37.

are some definite indications that the incumbents of this office were sometimes removable inasmuch as they possessed only a manual benefice. Thus a Council of Paris which was held in 1212 referred to both types.[38] Furthermore, a Decretal of Pope Innocent III (1198-1216) seems to indicate that the incumbent was removable from the office provided that the removal was executed by the joint action of the bishop and the archdeacon, since the rural deans exercised an office which in common pertained to them both.[39]

No explicit legislation can be found to the effect that those rural deans who were apparently constituted in office only temporarily could be removed in a simple manner without the need of a process or of a judicial sentence. Nevertheless it seems that, inasfar as they were temporary officials, the principle taught by the commentators, and as explained in the preceding section concerning the vicar general,[40] applied also to these temporary rural deans as well as to all other temporary vicars. Hence they could be removed *ad nutum* by the one who had constituted them in office, although at least, at the time of Pope Innocent III such a removal postulated the joint action of the bishop and the archdeacon.[41]

Article II. The Vicar Forane

Just when the term "vicar forane" began to be applied to the office of rural archpriest or rural dean is difficult to determine, as was stated above.[42] Zaplotnik points out that some authors re-

---

[38] Council of Paris (1212), c. 14: "Inhibemus etiam ne decanatus rurales ad tempus vel in perpetuum pro pecunia vel aliquo pretio alicui conferantur . . ."; —Mansi, XXII, 823.

[39] "Subsequenter postea quaesivisti, utrum decani rurales, qui pro tempore statuuntur, ad mandatum tuum solum, vel archidiaconi, vel etiam utriusque institui debeant vel destitui, si fuerint amovendi. Ad hos breviter respondemus, quod, ab omnibus quod omnes tangit approbari debeat, et quum commune eorum decanus officium exerceat, communiter est eligendus vel etiam amovendus."—c. 7, X, *de officio archidiaconi,* I, 23; Potthast, n. 5031.

[40] *Supra,* pp. 9-11.

[41] Schmalzgrueber, *Jus Ecclesiasticum Universum,* Lib. I, tit. 28, n. 1; *supra,* p. 15, where it was noted that a reasonable cause was demanded for the lawfulness of such a removal.

[42] *Supra,* p. 12.

garded it as certain that the vicars forane had made their appearance in Italy before 1542, but that many others held, and that many authors still hold, with Thomassinus (1619-1695) that St. Charles Borromeo, Cardinal and Archbishop of Milan (1560-1584), first introduced them.[43] Whatever be the exact origin, St. Charles certainly reformed the office after the Council of Trent.[44] This is clearly evident from the legislation of the I Council of Milan in 1565.[45]

SECTION IV. PAROCHIAL VICARS

Article I. Preliminary Notions

Other officials who were dealt with in pre-Tridentine legislation, and whose removal may be considered under the category of simple removal apart from any juridical process, may be grouped under the general title of parochial vicars. This title is now incorporated in the Code of Canon Law in Book II, Chapter X, Title VIII.

A parochial vicar may be defined as one "who in the name of the pastor and in his place exercises the parochial functions, that is, takes the pastor's place in the care of souls."[46]

The Code distinguishes five types or species of parochial vicars, in line with the various purposes for which the vicars are constituted. Accordingly there are the vicars of a moral person (also called perpetual or actual vicars),[47] the vicars econome (also called

---

[43] Zaplotnik, *De Vicariis Foraneis,* p. 41; Thomassinus, Pars I, lib. II, c. 6, n. 3.

[44] Cappello, *Summa Iuris Canonici* (3 vols., Vol. I, 4. ed., Romae: Apud Aedes Universitatis Gregorianae, 1945), I, 434: ". . . statuit [S. Carolus] autem ut iidem [vicarii foranei] *ad nutum Episcopi essent amovibiles*"; cf. De Meester, *op. cit.,* II, 238.

[45] "Hi autem vicarii voluntate episcopi ab officio amoveri semper possunt."—Mansi, XXXIVa, 43.

[46] De Meester, *Compendium,* II, 330: ". . . est vicarius in divinis, qui scilicet parochi nomine ejusque loco munera exercet parochialia, id est, vices ejus gerit in cura animarum et divinis ministeriis."

[47] De Meester, *op. cit.,* II, 331: "Vicarii personae moralis . . . sunt illi, qui canonice sunt institui ad exercendam curam actualem animarum, dum cura habitualis sit penes personam moralem cui pleno jure paroecia est unita. . . . Cf. also canon 471, § 1.

administrators in the United States),[48] the vicars substitute,[49] the vicars adjutant,[50] and finally the vicars assistant (*vicarii cooperatores*), commonly known as assistant pastors.

Of these vicars, some enjoy ordinary jurisdiction, others only delegated jurisdiction. Concerning some the authors dispute as to which type of jurisdiction is possessed by them.[51]

Article II. The Removal of the Perpetual Vicar

The perpetual vicar (*vicarius actualis*) was appointed at parishes which had been attached in title to some moral person, e.g., to a monastery or to a collegiate church. Thus the moral person held title to the parish, but the vicar exercised the actual parochial care inherent in that title.

During the later Middle Ages certain abuses had crept in, among which was the appointment of temporary vicars to parochial churches, or to parishes which were attached to a monastery, so that the vicar could be removed at will by the monks themselves or the patrons. Sufficient legislation can be cited from synods, from councils, and also from the Decretals, in order to show that definite steps were taken to correct these abuses, so that the removal of the vicar was no longer to be an arbitrary matter. Quite to the contrary, the vicar was to be constituted as a perpetual vicar.

---

[48] De Meester, *op. cit.,* II, 332: "Vicarii oeconomi sunt illi, qui *vacante* quacumque ex causa parochia, ad regendam parochiam deputantur, donec novus parochus constituatur." Cf. also canon 472, 1°.

[49] De Meester, *op. cit.,* II, 334: "Vicarius substitutus ille est qui legitime constituendus est ut in cura animarum vices gerat parochi qui ultra hebdomadam vel a paroecia, praevia obtenta licentia, discedit vel ab ea repentina causa abesse cogitur, aut qui privatus suo beneficio sententia judiciali, ad Sanctam Sedem appellavit." Cf. also canons 474; 465, §§ 4, 5; 1923, § 2.

[50] De Meester, *op. cit.,* II, 336: "Coadjutor parochi stricte dictus est sacerdos, Ordinarii auctoritate deputatus, ad vices supplendum parochi qui ob senectutem, mentis vitium, imperitiam, caecitatem aliamve permanentem causam, non amplius convenienter regere potest parochiam ipsi commissam." Cf. also canon 475.

[51] The historical survey will be limited to those offices which have attached to them ordinary jurisdiction. A more complete discussion of the application of canon 192, § 3, to offices whose incumbents possess only delegated power will be given below in the canonical commentary. Cf. *infra,* pp. 80-91.

Thus, as early as 1096 the Council of Nîmes ruled that priests who were placed over churches to exercise the care of souls were to serve God in those churches permanently, unless they were degraded after a canonical trial.[52] In the next century, a council held at Rheims legislated against the abuse of committing the care of churches to hired vicars.[53] The II General Council of the Lateran (1139) confirmed this statute.[54]

In the Decretal legislation there is definite evidence that at the time of Pope Alexander III (1159-1181) a perpetual vicar, when appointed to a church or a benefice with the assent and authority of the bishop, could not be removed by the moral person which held the parish in title, unless he had committed some wrong for which he was condemned by a judge.[55] Likewise Pope Urban III (1185-1187) ordered that the churches of monks were to be governed by pastors or vicars whom the monks had presented to the bishop for approval, but whom the monks themselves could not afterwards remove, since that power was reserved to the bishop.[56] The Glossator observed that the monks could not remove the vicar. In the event of the latter's delinquency he was to be removed by the bishop in a judiciary manner.[57]

This principle regarding the perpetual vicar was confirmed by the teaching of Pope Innocent III (1189-1216) in the IV General Council of the Lateran (1215), wherein he decreed that those who held prebends or dignities as offices in addition to their possession

[52] Council of Nîmes (1096), c. 9—Mansi, XX, 936; Connor, *The Administrative Removal of Pastors,* p. 9.

[53] Council of Rheims (1131), c. 9: "Placuit etiam ne in conductiis presbyteris ecclesiae committantur."—Mansi, XXI, 460.

[54] II General Council of the Lateran (1139), c. 10—Mansi, XXI, 569.

[55] C. 3, X, *de officio vicarii,* I, 28: ". . . nisi aliquid committat, propter quod per iudicem in vicaria sit vel beneficio condemnandus." Cf. Jaffé, n. 14156.

[56] C. I, X, *de capellis monachorum et aliorum religiosorum,* III, 37: "In ecclesiis ubi monachi habitant, populus per monachum non regatur, sed capellanus qui populum regat, ab episcopo per consilium monachorum instituatur; ita ut ex solius episcopi arbitrio, tum ordinatio eius, quam depositio, et totius vitae pendeat conversatio." Cf. also Thomassinus, Pars I, lib. II, cap. 27, n. 9, who says that even the bishop could not remove him except by means of a canonical trial.

[57] *Glossa Ord.,* ad. c. I, X, *de capellis monachorum et aliorum religiosorum,* III, 37, s.v. *solius.*

of the parochial office were to have a suitable and perpetual vicar canonically instituted in the parochial church.[58]

With good reason, therefore, did Reiffenstuel note, in his commentary on the Decretal of Pope Innocent III, that the perpetual vicar could not be removed *ad libitum,* since he held title to his vicarial office as a permanent incumbent, so that once he was canonically instituted he could not be removed unless he had committed some crime which called for his deposition or his deprivation of the benefice.[59] Temporary vicars, on the other hand, were those who, on the authority of the legitimate superior, were appointed in the place of another for a time, and who could be removed *ad nutum* by the one who had appointed them.[60]

Thus, too, was exemplified again the essential difference between a manual and a non-manual benefice, since, as Schmalzgrueber (1663-1735) explained, the incumbent of the non-manual benefice, once he was legitimately constituted, could not be removed except for a just cause which was directly mentioned in the law.[61]

It may incidentally be noted here that the same legislation was continued by the Council of Trent, which enacted the general rule that vicars should be assigned permanently to churches, but at the same time with relation to the exceptional case allowed for the institution of vicars removable *ad nutum,* that is, whenever necessity demanded it.[62]

---

[58] C. 30, X, *de praebendis et dignitatibus,* III, 5: ". . . qui talem habet praebendam vel dignitatem, cum oporteat eum in maiori ecclesia deservire, in ipsa parochiali ecclesia idoneum et perpetuum habeat vicarium, canonice institutum . . ."; Mansi, XXII, 1019.

[59] Reiffenstuel, Lib. I, tit. 28, nn. 22-24.

[60] *Ibidem,* n. 25.

[61] Schmalzgrueber, *Jus Ecclesiasticum Universum,* Lib. III, tit. 5, n. 34: "non-manuale . . . quod confertur in titulum perpetuum, ita, ut semel legitime collatum beneficiato, nisi ex justa, et jure expressa causa, auferri nequeat." Concerning the manual benefice, cf. *supra,* p. 10, footnote n. 28; p. 11.

[62] Conc. Trident., sess. VII, *de ref.,* c. 7: "Beneficia ecclesiastica curata, quae cathedralibus seu collegiis aut piis locis quibuscumque perpetuo unita et annexa reperiuntur ab Ordinariis locorum annis singulis visitentur; qui sollicite providere procurent, ut per idoneos vicarios, etiam perpetuos, nisi ipsis Ordinariis pro bono ecclesiarum regimine aliter expedire videbitur . . . animarum cura exerceatur"; Connor, *The Administrative Removal of Pastors,* p. 9; Galvin, *The Administrative Transfer of Pastors,* The Catholic University of America Canon Law Studies, n. 232 (Washington, D. C.: The Catholic University of America Press, 1946), p. 26.

Article III. The Removal of the Temporary Vicar

Regarding the removal of the other parochial vicars mentioned above, that is, the vicar econome (administrator), the vicar substitute, the vicar adjutant, and the vicar assistant, the immediate and primary concern is with the vicar econome, the vicar substitute, and the vicar adjutant in so far as these supplied for the pastor in all things and therefore enjoyed full parochial rights and duties.

The principle underlying the removal from office of these vicars has already been brought to light in the preceding pages. For (whether they enjoyed ordinary or delegated power of jurisdiction), in so far as they were temporary vicars by the very nature of their offices, they could be removed *ad nutum* by the one who had constituted them in their office.[63] At most they possessed a manual benefice, and hence their tenure was temporary, and as incumbents they were removable at the will of the bishop or of their legitimate superior.[64] However, it must be emphasized again that a reasonable cause was required for the lawfulness of the removal of these vicars, just as for the removal of the other temporary vicars already considered.[65]

---

[63] *Supra,* p. 11.

[64] *Supra,* pp. 9-11.

[65] *Supra,* p. 11. Since this work is concerned with the power of the ordinary to remove incumbents from manual offices for a just or reasonable cause, but apart from the need of any process, the reader is referred to the work of Bastnagel concerning the power which pastors at one time enjoyed, namely, of removing adjutant and assistant vicars. Cf. Bastnagel, *The Appointment of Parochial Adjutants and Assistants,* The Catholic University of America Canon Law Studies, n. 58 (Washington, D. C.: The Catholic University of America Press, 1930), p. 72.

CHAPTER II

The Law Regarding Simple Removal From Office From the Council of Trent to the Code of Canon Law

Section I. The Council of Trent

It may be noted in general that very little legislation is to be found regarding the simple removal from office from the time of the Council of Trent until the Code of Canon Law. The principle involved in such an act of removal appeared to be so well established by that time that there was little need for any further legislation. The Council of Trent therefore did not concern itself directly with the question of removal from office, whether administrative or simple. There were however some indirect confirmations of the principle involved in the act of simple removal in so far as the Council recognized the existence or allowed for the possible appointment of temporary vicars who enjoyed parochial powers and rights.

The Council of Trent enacted the general rule that perpetual vicars should be assigned to churches which called for the appointment of vicars, but it also allowed for the assignment of vicars who were removable *ad nutum,* that is, whenever necessity demanded such an exception to the general rule.[1]

Such at least is the interpretation given by Reiffenstuel for the words of the Council "... *nisi ipsis Ordinariis pro bono ecclesiarum regimine aliter expedire videbitur.*"[2] The same author pointed to cases wherein, according to the decree of the Council of Trent, the bishop could not constitute a perpetual vicar. Such a case was verified, for example, when it had been the custom from time immemorial with the knowledge and consent of the ordinaries to

---

[1] Conc. Trident., sess. VII, *de ref.,* c. 7; cf. *supra,* p. 27, footnote n. 62.

[2] Conc. Trident., sess. VII, *de ref.,* c. 7; Reiffenstuel, Lib. III, tit. 28, nn. 27-28: ". . . tunc sufficit instituere Vicarium temporalem, et ad nutum amovibilem."

constitute temporary vicars in certain parochial churches. The same kind of exceptional procedure was applicable when for the good of peace and the cessation of litigations it seemed expedient that nothing be innovated, so that there would be appointed a vicar who was *ad nutum* removable.

The twenty-fourth session of the Council of Trent was concerned in part with the right and duty of bishops to make the episcopal visitation of their diocese. After stating clearly the purpose of these visitations, the Council, to enable the bishops to carry out that purpose, enacted that they had the right "to decree, regulate, punish and execute, in accordance with the prescriptions of the canons, those things which in their prudence shall appear to them necessary for the emendation of the subjects and for the good of their dioceses."[3] Though it was a very general statement, yet this enactment appears in principle to have included for the bishops the power to remove those who held manual benefices or offices from which they were removable by a simple decree of the bishop. The principle which had been established before the Council of Trent seems nowhere to have been abrogated by that Council.

In the same session, moreover, the Council decreed that when a parochial church became vacant it was the duty of the bishop to appoint immediately a competent vicar—with a suitable assignment of a portion of the income—who was to discharge the duties in that church till it had been provided with a pastor.[4] Hence the vicar who was thus appointed, and who enjoyed full parochial powers and rights, was evidently a temporary vicar inasmuch as at any time he could be called on to yield his place to the newly appointed pastor.

Finally, in the twenty-fifth and final session of the Council allowance was made for the fact of the appointment of removable vicars to monastic churches if there was annexed to them the *cura animarum* of secular persons. The Council of Trent decreed that no one, not even such as were removable *ad nutum*, could be

---

[3] Conc. Trident., sess. XXIV, *de ref.*, c. 10; Schroeder, *Canons and Decrees of the Council of Trent* (St. Louis: B. Herder Book Co., 1941), p. 468.

[4] Conc. Trident., sess. XXIV, *de ref.*, c. 18.

appointed to these monastic churches except with the consent of the bishop and after having been examined by him or his vicar.[5]

SECTION II. ORDINANCES OF THE POPES AND OF THE SACRED ROMAN CONGREGATIONS

For the period following the Council of Trent down to the Code of Canon Law some applications of the law in particular cases as also the clarification of doubtful points were responsible for whatever further ordinances can be found in the writings of the Popes and in the decrees and responses of the Sacred Roman Congregations.

Article I. Typical Causes for Removal

Some reasonable or just causes aside from strict canonical causes for the removal of the vicar general were indicated in the seventeenth century in decrees emanating from the Sacred Congregation of Bishops and Regulars as listed by Ferraris (+ ca. 1763). While these causes were designated as applicable specifically to the office of the vicar general, they were in the same way applicable to any and all of the incumbents of offices who were subject to a simple removal from office for a just and reasonable cause.

Before listing the causes for removal, Ferraris stated that the vicar general could be removed at the will of the bishop—*ad libitum Episcopi.* But he was careful to insist that in such an act of removal consideration had always to be given to the honor of the vicar; the removal had to be effected with great circumspection, and for a grave and just cause, otherwise the vicar general could be reinstated in his office through the Sacred Congregation of Bishops and Regulars.[6]

Among the just causes for which a vicar general could be re-

---

[5] Conc. Trident., sess. XXV, *de regularibus,* c. 2: "Nec ibi aliqui etiam ad nutum amovibiles deputentur, nisi de ejusdem [episcopi] consensu, ac praevio examine per eum aut ejus vicarium faciendo."

[6] Ferraris, s.v. *Vicarius Generalis,* nn. 28-38. The author based his teaching on two decisions of the Sacred Roman Congregation of Bishops and Regulars: S.C. Ep. et Reg., *Spalaten.,* 3 iul. 1610; *Tragurien.,* 7 sept. et 8 oct. 1649.

moved, Ferraris noted the following cases as worthy of special mention: 1) if many complaints were heard about the vicar;[7] 2) if the vicar general was deficient in his rule and government, or if he did not inform the Sacred Congregation about causes of great importance in the event that the bishop neglected this duty or was absent from the diocese;[8] 3) if he wrote irreverently to the Sacred Congregation and its officials;[9] 4) if he did not treat the Cardinals of the Church with the reverence that was due them;[10] 5) if he lacked circumspection and prudence, even though he was fit for the office in other respects;[11] 6) if he became subject to excommunication;[12] and 7) if he refused to obey the commands of the Sacred Congregation.[13]

It should be noted here that the presence of such and similar just causes was required not for the validity of the act of removal, but for the lawfulness, as Wernz (1842-1914) clearly maintained.[14]

Article II. The Removal of Religious Pastors

The pastors here dealt with are those who receive mention in canon 454, § 5, of the Code, that is, pastors who belong to religious communities and who, as far as their individual person is concerned, are always removable both at the will of the bishop and also at the will of their respective religious superior.[15]

---

[7] S.C. Ep. et Reg., *Spalaten.*, 5 febr. 1601—Ferraris, *loc. cit.*

[8] S.C. Ep. et Reg., *Agrigentinen.* et *Tranen.*, 3 dec. 1601—Ferraris, *loc. cit.*

[9] S.C. Ep. et Reg., *Reatina,* 3 sept. 1601—Ferraris, *loc. cit.*

[10] S.C. Ep. et Reg., *Savonen.*, 19 nov. 1655—Ferraris, *loc. cit.*

[11] S.C. Ep. et Reg., *Placentina,* 11 sept. 1601—Ferraris, *loc. cit.*

[12] S.C. Ep. et Reg., *Placentina,* 18 iun. 1649—Ferraris, *loc. cit.*

[13] S.C. Ep. et Reg. *Parmen.*, 17 aug. 1649—Ferraris, *loc. cit.*

[14] *Ius Decretalium,* II, n. 806: "Potestas Vicarii generalis praeter ipsius mortem cessat per *revocationem* mandati expressam vel tacitam ab Episcopo etiam sine causa *valide* factam; at ut *licite* fiat, ratio habenda est *honoris* Vicarii generalis et *iusta gravisque causa* intercedat necesse est; secus Vicarius generalis ad salvandum honorem recurrere potest ad S.C., ut sibi per redintegrationem vel alium convenientem modum consulat."

[15] Canon 454, § 5.—Parochi autem, ad religiosam familiam pertinentes, sunt semper, ratione personae, amovibiles ad nutum tam loci Ordinarii, monito Superiore, quam Superioris, monito Ordinario, aequo iure, non requisito alterius consensu: nec alter alteri causam iudicii sui aperire multoque minus probare tenetur, salvo recursu in devolutivo ad Apostolicam Sedem.

As early as 1655 the Sacred Congregation of Bishops and Regulars was asked whether, in the light of Pope Innocent X's Constitution *Ut in parvis* (Feb. 10, 1654), which was concerned with the subjection of religious churches to the visitation and jurisdiction of the local ordinary as a delegate of the Holy See, the bishop could remove the religious from these churches when they had the care of souls attached to them. The Sacred Congregation, after first having suggested to the proper regular superior that he assign them to other churches, answered that the bishop could remove them for a reasonable cause.[16] Again on September 11, 1670, the same Sacred Congregation ruled that the regular superiors themselves could in their churches which had the care of souls nominate vicars to exercise that care, and could also remove these vicars and pastors at their will (*ad nutum*), if the local ordinary had from the beginning deputed them as removable.[17]

Similar legislation regarding the removal of these religious or regular pastors was enacted through the Sacred Congregation of the Council. Thus on September 18, 1627, the same Sacred Congregation decreed that a monk exercising the care of souls in a church united to a monastery was removable at the will of the bishop, so that it was not necessary for the bishop to disclose the reasons for the removal or to vindicate them.[18] That the religious superior also enjoyed a degree of independence with reference to manifesting the cause or reason for which he undertook to remove a pastor subject to him is evident from the affirmative answer of the same Sacred Congregation (July 13, 1669) to the Bishop of Narni, who had inquired whether a regular pastor, when nominated by his superior and approved by the bishop, could be removed at the will of the same superior, apart from

[16] Innocentius X, const. *Ut in parvis,* 10 febr. 1654—*Bullarum Diplomatum et Privilegiorum Sanctorum Romanorum Pontificum Taurinensis Editio* (24 vols. et Appendix, Augustae Taurinorum, 1857-1872), XV, 754 (hereafter cited as *Bull. Rom.*) ; S.C. Ep. et Reg., 27 iul. 1655—*Codicis Iuris Canonici Fontes cura Emi Card. Gasparri editi* (9 vols., Romae [postea Civitate Vaticana] : Typis Polyglottis Vaticanis, 1923-1939), n. 1791 (hereafter cited as *Fontes*).

[17] S.C. Ep. et *Reg.,* declar. 11 sept. 1670—*Fontes,* n. 1803.

[18] S.C.C., *Camerinen.,* 18 sept. 1627—*Fontes,* n. 2484.

any need of asking the bishop, even when the cause of the removal had not been previously approved by the bishop.[19]

Moreover, some indication as to the wide scope of the cause for which these pastors could be removed at the will of the proper religious superior is given in an answer of December 17, 1689. The Sacred Congregation of the Council ruled that the Father General of the Order of Carmelites could lawfully remove those pastors who were subject to his jurisdiction and appointed by him with the approval of the ordinary, howsoever and whensoever the utility and benefit either of the religious institute or of the Church demanded it, and whenever it seemed expedient to the Father General to effect their removal.[20]

However, that the bishop was to be notified of such removals by the religious superiors was insisted on in an answer given to the Bishop of Passau on July 28, 1731, when the question was raised by the Abbot of the Monastery of Aldersbach.[21]

Finally, mention may be made of a declaration of the Sacred Congregation for the Propagation of the Faith on August 8, 1698, to the effect that it was not lawful for a vicar apostolic to take churches away from regulars. Nevertheless, he could for a legitimate cause remove any religious, provided that another, who was to be deputed by the vicar apostolic, was then put in the place of the one who had been removed.[22]

Practically all the foregoing ordinances were repeated and confirmed by Pope Benedict XIV in the Constitution *Firmandis,* on November 6, 1744. Among other matters the Pontiff considered the removal of religious pastors who had charge of parochial churches which were attached to the monasteries of regulars. These pastors were removable *ad nutum,* the Pope pointed out. He approved and confirmed the teaching of the Sacred Congregation of the Council to the effect that such pastors could be removed both by the bishop and by the regular superior, each having an equal right in this matter, so that neither had to have the previous consent of the other, and neither had to disclose to the other the causes

[19] S.C.C., *Narnien.,* 13 iul. 1669, ad I—*Fontes,* n. 2813.

[20] S.C.C., 17 dec. 1689—*Fontes,* n. 2915.

[21] S.C.C., *Passavien.,* 28 iul. 1731, ad 3—*Fontes,* n. 3373.

[22] S.C. de Prop. Fide (C.P. pro Sin.), 8 aug. 1698—*Fontes,* n. 4492.

for his action, much less to prove and vindicate them.[23] It should be noted that the Pope did not maintain that neither the bishop nor the superior needed to have a cause for the removal, but simply that neither had to disclose this cause to the other, or to prove and vindicate it.

This teaching of Pope Benedict XIV set the standard for settling future doubts and difficulties on the question of the removal of religious pastors. In fact, in two instances the Sacred Congregation for the Propagation of the Faith, in response to questions sent to it regarding the removal of pastors who belonged to a religious institute, answered that the norm as confirmed in the Constitution *Firmandis* was to be followed.[24]

SECTION III. JURISPRUDENCE OF THE HOLY SEE CONCERNING THE ACT OF SIMPLE REMOVAL FROM OFFICE

Additional light is thrown on the question of simple removal, and on the principle involved in such a removal, especially from the point of view of the cause required for a simple removal or a removal made *ad nutum,* from a consideration of the jurisprudence of the Holy See. This jurisprudence is contained in part at least in certain decrees of the Sacred Congregation of the Council and in the publication, the *Acta Sanctae Sedis.*

Thus on July 27, 1867, the Sacred Congregation of the Council ruled concerning the removal of chaplains or assistants that,

---

[23] Benedictus XIV, const. *Firmandis,* 6 nov. 1744, § 11: ". . . quoniam huiusmodi Parochis, sine praevia Episcopi approbatione, ad curam animarum accedere nequaquam licet, quamvis a suis Superioribus deputati, iidemque ad nutum sint amovibiles; dubitatum propterea fuit, an Episcopus posset ad huiusmodi remotiones procedere, sine Superioris Regularis consensu, et an remotionis causas eidem adducere, easque verificare deberet; tum etiam an Regularis Superior ad similem remotionem et privationem suo iure deveniens, consensum Episcopi exquirere, suasque agendi rationes illi notas atque probatas facere teneretur. Qua de re . . . Congregatio Concilii decrevit, huiusmodi Parochos tam ab Episcopo, quam a Superiore Regulari, aequo iure, non requisito alterius consensu, ab animarum cura removeri posse, nec unum alteri causas iudicii sui aperire, multoque minus probare et verificare debere. Id quod a Nobis in omnibus approbatur et confirmatur."—*Fontes,* n. 349.

[24] S.C. de Prop. Fide (C.G.), 13 maii 1839—*Fontes,* n. 4779; S.C. de Prop. Fide (C.G.), 18 ian. 1886, ad 3—*Fontes,* n. 4913.

according to canonical equity and ecclesiastical discipline, it was not expedient that these removable chaplains be removed without any cause, inasmuch as a removal without any cause for the most part injured the honor of the one removed and disturbed good order.[25]

That same year, in a commentary on the removability of clerics from offices, the editors of the *Acta Sanctae Sedis* in recounting the historical development regarding offices and benefices pointed out that, in spite of the fact that ecclesiastical discipline had consistently demanded that those who possessed benefices could not be removed without a canonical cause or apart from a canonical procedure, there came to be instituted in the Church certain offices whose incumbents, in contradistinction to the general nature of the ecclesiastical discipline, were appointed as removable incumbents.[26]

The editors then proceeded to explain the removability of the incumbents of those offices which lacked subjective perpetuity, either simply, or *ad nutum*, or *ad beneplacitum* of the superior who had made the appointment to the office. They contended that, in accordance with the general canonical discipline of the Church, removability was to be understood not in an absolute sense but in a relative sense. This, they explained, meant that, although the incumbents could be removed even in the absence of any specific cause or of any procedural form as postulated in the law, nevertheless they could not be removed in the absence of every equitable and reasonable cause, for there had to be present a cause which, though canonically not designated as a cause, nevertheless corresponded to the demand of equity and to the manifest tenor of the law's solicitude for fairness as expressed in the sacred canons. For nothing, so the editors continued, was so foreign to the spirit of the Church, which is a most orderly society, as an arbitrariness which is not put to use even over one's domestic servants.[27]

---

[25] S.C.C., 27 iul. 1867: ". . . remotio enim sine causa plerumque honorem laedit ordinemque perturbat," as found in the *Acta Sanctae Sedis* (41 vols., Romae, 1865-1908), III (1867), 457 (hereafter cited *ASS*).

[26] *ASS*, III (1867), 510.

[27] ". . . quare apparet Clericorum amovibilitatem a propriis constitutis officiis generatim consideratam, accipi non posse sensu absoluto, sed dumtaxat sensu relativo: ex quo consequitur, quamvis eos amoveri possint sine causa

In a response of March 23, 1878, the Sacred Congregation of the Council answered concerning the removable pastors in France, called *desservants,* that such pastors could be regarded as on an equal basis with the possessors of manual benefices, or even with vicars who had the *cura animarum* as incumbents removable *ad nutum Episcopi,* and therefore that the general rule applied, namely, that inasmuch as the bishops had freely conferred these parishes, they could also freely and even without cause remove or transfer the rectors. However, the application of this general rule was subject to a limitation. The removal was never to be undertaken: 1) if it was motivated solely out of hatred; 2) if it implied exclusively the loss of the incumbent's reputation or any notable harm or detriment to the priest who was removed or transferred; and 3) if it resulted in preventable damage to a third party. Yet, there could readily exist sufficiently grave causes that more than counterbalanced even these limitations as related considerations. Accordingly the Congregation concluded that in practice there was scarcely admissible any case of removal which was not based on some reasonable cause. Hence, regarding the removal of these pastors one had to maintain what applied to the possessors of manual benefices, that is, even though in theory such pastors were removable *ad nutum* by the ordinary, nevertheless some cause, at least a reasonable one, was always necessary that the removal might be undertaken lawfully.[28]

On August 24, 1878, the Sacred Congregation of the Council repeated its teaching that the simple fact of a vicar's removability from his office did not justify the conclusion that the vicar could be removed apart from the presence of any cause. A just and reasonable cause was required, even though that cause did not need to be one of grave importance. Moreover, the juridical procedure which had to be observed when there was question of re-

---

et forma canonice praescripta, propter indolem fundationum ab Ecclesia admissam, tamen non posse amoveri sine honesta rationabilique causa; quae etsi canonice non sit praescripta, sit tamen juxta aequitatem et indolem ss. canonum; nihil enim est a spiritu Ecclesiae tam alienum, quae ordinatissima societas est, quam arbitrium, quo neque in domesticos servos uti solemus."—*ASS,* III (1867), 510-511.

[28] *ASS,* XI (1878), 392-393.

moving one who had a title to a benefice as an irremovable incumbent could be foregone.[29]

The same teaching, based on the distinction between a manual benefice and a benefice granted in perpetuity, was reiterated in a decision of the Sacred Roman Rota on April 5, 1916, in settlement of a case sent from Buenos Aires.[30] The decision referred to the teaching of such authors as Barbosa (1589-1649), Gonzalez-Tellez (+ after 1673) and Reiffenstuel (1642-1703), and to three earler decisions of the Rota, namely on April 20, 1640, June 21, 1641, and June 22, 1642. After restating the common teaching that one who had the right could remove the incumbent of a manual benefice even without a cause, provided that no malice or hatred was involved in the act of removal, the Rota added the qualification that, since every act of ecclesiastical administration must be prudent, some reasonable cause was required for the lawfulness of the act of removal, though the act was to be regarded as valid even apart from the existence of such a cause.

SECTION IV. REMOVABLE PASTORS IN THE UNITED STATES BEFORE THE CODE OF CANON LAW

In the dioceses of the United States of America there were definitely pastors of the secular clergy who were removable *ad nutum*. At the time of the first bishop of the new nation, Bishop John Carroll (1789-1815), distinct parishes were not known. Even after his time the bishops carried on the care of their whole diocese through priests sent out from the cathedral church to the various parts of the cities and of the diocese; these priests were removable *ad nutum Episcopi*.[31]

But in the course of time, with the increase of the Catholic population, the need was felt for a more stable, and indeed a more canonical, arrangement based on a closer observance of the regula-

---

[29] S.C.C., 24 aug. 1878—*ASS,* XII (1878), 283.

[30] S.R.R., decis. *Bonaëren. Remotionis,* 5 apr. 1916, *coram Gulielmo Sebastianelli, Decano—Acta Apostolicae Sedis* (Romae, 1909-), IX (1917, 85-93 (hereafter cited *AAS*).

[31] *Acta et Decreta Concilii Plenarii Baltimorensis Tertii A.D. MDCCCLXXXIV* (Baltimorae: Typis Joannis Murphy et Sociorum, 1886), n. 31.

tions of the Council of Trent with regard to parishes and their rectors. Accordingly the Fathers of the II Plenary Council of Baltimore (1866) decreed that throughout the provinces, especially in the larger cities where there were several churches, a certain district after the manner of a parish with accurately defined boundaries was to be assigned to each church, and that parochial or quasi-parochial rights were to be acknowledged for its rector. But they added that by such action they in no way intended to make these rectors irremovable or to take away or lessen in any way the power which the bishop had of removing any priest from his office or of transferring him to another. However, the conciliar decree advised and exhorted the bishops not to use this right except for grave causes.[32]

Finally, in order to strengthen ecclesiastical discipline and reform in this matter a little further, the Fathers of the III Plenary Council of Baltimore in 1884 enacted legislation to the effect that in each diocese by the authority of the bishop and with the advice of the diocesan consultors there were to be designated certain missions which were to be ruled over by rectors who were permanently instituted as irremovable incumbents. But these irremovable rectors were not to exceed a tenth part of all the rectors of a given diocese, so that the rest remained removable *ad nutum.*[33]

Upon the enactment of the famous decree *Maxima cura* of August 20, 1910, which gave the norms for the administrative removal of pastors,[34] the question was asked of the Holy See whether this decree was binding also for the dioceses of the United States. To this question the Sacred Congregation of the Consistory gave an affirmative reply on March 13, 1911, as it had done on February 28th of the same year for the dioceses of England.[35]

---

[32] "Monemus autem et hortamur ne Episcopi hoc iure suo, nisi graves ob causas et habita meritorum ratione, uti velint."—*Concilii Plenarii Baltimorensis II, in Ecclesia Metropolitana Baltimorensi, a die VII ad diem XXI Octobris, A.D. MDCCCLXVI, Habiti, et a Sede Apostolica Recogniti, Acta et Decreta* (Baltimorae: John Murphy, 1868), n. 125.

[33] *Acta et Decreta,* n. 35.

[34] S.C. Consist., decr. *Maxima cura,* 20 aug. 1910—*AAS,* II (1910), 647; *Fontes,* n. 2074.

[35] S.C. Consist., 13 mart. 1911—*AAS,* III (1911), 133.

However, canon 30 of the decree *Maxima cura* had indeed stated that the norms of the decrees were to be applied to all who had a parish by any title as its proper rector, whether they were called perpetual vicars, or *desservants* (in France), or by any other name, but that these norms were not to be applied in the removal of those to whom a parish was committed in their capacity of *"oeconomi temporales"* (called administrators in the United States), or of *"vicarii ad tempus,"* whether in view of the pastor's incapacity through sickness or infirmity, or in consequence of the vacancy in the benefice, or for some other similar consideration.[36] Hence, on the basis that the norms of the decree were to be applied to all who had a parish by any title as its proper rector, some thought that there were included in this class also the rectors of the parishes or of the missions which in the United States according to the decrees of the III Plenary Council of Baltimore (1886) still were ruled by removable pastors. The doubt which thus rose was sent to the Holy See for a solution. The Sacred Congregation of the Consistory replied that the rules, and especially canon 30, of the decree *Maxima cura* did not apply to these removable pastors, and that they could still be removed *ad nutum Episcopi.* But the admonition of the II Plenary Council of Baltimore (1866) was acknowledged as remaining in force, namely, that the bishops were not to use their right except for grave reasons and only after mature consideration of the demands inherent in the case.[37]

Some of the arguments given by the Sacred Congregation for this answer were the following. The purpose of the decree *Maxima cura* would not be obtained if its regulations were to be applied to those who by nature are removable *ad nutum Ordinarii,* for in that event the manner of the removal, which could lend itself to easy and prompt execution, would be made more difficult and complicated. Furthermore, according to canon 30 of the decree, the regulations were to be applied to those who had obtained parishes in the capacity of being their *proper* rectors. But those who ad-

[36] S.C. Consist., decr. *Maxima cura,* 20 aug. 1910, can. 30—*AAS,* II (1910), 647; *Fontes,* n. 2074.

[37] S.C. Consist., *Statuum Foederatorum Americae Septentrionalis,* 28 ian. 1915—*AAS,* VII (1915), 378-382; Connor, *The Administrative Removal of Pastors,* p. 45.

ministered parishes *ad nutum Ordinarii* could evidently not be regarded as the proper pastors of the parishes where they labored. Therefore the decree *Maxima cura* made no change with regard to the manner of removal of all those pastors who had not been assigned as irremovable incumbents. This change was in fact to come only with the Code of Canon Law.[38]

---

[38] Galvin, *The Administrative Transfer of Pastors*, p. 31.

PART TWO

Canonical Commentary

CHAPTER III

INTRODUCTORY NOTIONS

Most of the material contained in this chapter has already been treated in previous dissertations. However, for a proper understanding of the nature of the simple removal from office, a repetition, at least of the main notions, seems warranted. Therefore due consideration will be given to the notion of an ecclesiastical office, and to the types of removal from office with which the Code of Canon Law is concerned.

SECTION I. THE NOTION OF AN ECCLESIASTICAL OFFICE

The Code treats the subject of ecclesiastical offices in canons 145-195, wherein are contained the general norms concerning offices, their provision and their loss. In the very first canon a distinction is made between an ecclesiastical office in the broad sense and in the strict sense. The former is defined as "quodlibet munus quod in finem spiritualem legitime exercetur."[1] Hence no special power, either of orders or of jurisdiction, is required for an office in the broad sense. Any charge exercised according to the norms of law for the glory of God and the good of souls is sufficient to constitute such an office.[2] Thus the bishop's secretary, the superioress of religious, professors, catechists, sacristans—all have an office in the broad sense.

The present work, however, is concerned with the removal from an office which is and must be considered as such in the strict sense alone. For the Code, in canon 145, § 2, clearly states that in law an ecclesiastical office is taken in the strict sense, unless the

---

[1] Canon 145, § 1.

[2] Cf. McDevitt, *The Renunciation of An Ecclesiastical Office,* The Catholic University of America Canon Law Studies, n. 218 (Washington, D. C.: The Catholic University of America Press, 1946), p. 2; Beste, *Introductio in Codicem* (2. ed., Collegeville, Minn.: St. John's Abbey Press, 1944), p. 197.

context indicates the contrary.[3] But there is no such indication in canon 192, the fundamental canon of this work.

The definition of an ecclesiastical office in the strict sense is in the words of the Code:

> . . . *munus ordinatione sive divina sive ecclesiastica stabiliter constitutum, ad normam sacrorum canonum conferendum, aliquem saltem secumferens participationem ecclesiasticae potestatis sive ordinis sive iurisdictionis.*[4]

An office in the strict sense is no longer defined as a grade of jurisdiction, but is called a *munus,* that is, a post, an employment, or a charge.[5] The concept is widened to include within its scope not only jurisdiction but also any kind of an ecclesiastical position with power other than jurisdiction which, as the definition itself states, includes a participation in the power of orders.

An office in the strict sense must possess the following qualifications or elements:

1) Institution by divine or ecclesiastical authority (*ordinatione sive divina sive ecclesiastica . . . constitutum*).—Some offices, as the papacy and the episcopate, are of divine origin; others, like the offices of the vicar general and the pastor, are of ecclesiastical origin. It is to be noted, as Maroto (1875-1937) explained, that there is question here not of the constitution of an ecclesiastical position in a definite place (*in specie*), but rather of the constitution of the position or office in its generic form (*in genere*).[6]

Thus, for example, the office of vicar general has been constituted by ecclesiastical authority as an office extant universally in

---

[3] "In iure officium ecclesiasticum accipitur stricto sensu, nisi aliud ex contextu sermonis appareat."

[4] Canon 145, § 1.

[5] The reader is referred to a pre-Code definition of an ecclesiastical office in the strict sense as defined by Wernz: ". . . gradus quidam iurisdictionis ecclesiasticae quoad personas, causas, locum legibus Christi vel Ecclesiae in perpetuum ita institutus, ut iura et onera spiritualia ipsi adnexa nomine proprio et ratione quadam stabili sint exercenda."—*Ius Decretalium,* II, n. 240.

[6] Maroto, *Institutiones Iuris Canonici* (2 vols., Vol. I, 3. ed., Romae: Apud Commentarium pro Religiosis, 1921), I, n. 582 (hereafter this work will be cited as *Institutiones*).

the Church. That is the constitution of the office *in genere*. The individual vicars general are appointed or constituted by diocesan ecclesiastical authority. As McBride explains, usually the Holy See establishes the office in the common law, and then the office is multiplied by an inferior, that is, diocesan authority. The law itself usually determines the kind of office, the limits of its powers, the circumstances and conditions under which it is to be multiplied *in specie*.[7] It should be added here that it would be possible however for an inferior ecclesiastical authority, e.g., a bishop, to constitute *in genere* a new office not already constituted by the common law, but merely for his own territory. Such an office could then be multiplied *in specie* either by himself or by others to whom the proper authority would be given.[8]

2) Stability (*stabiliter constitutum*).—This stability, all the authors agree, is an objective stability which applies to the office itself, and not to the incumbent's tenure of office.[9]

But objective stability does not demand that each specific multiplication of an office be of permanent constitution.[10] The administrator or vicar econome of a vacant parish is one instance, as reflected in the Code, of an office which in its generic constitution is stable, and thus fulfills the requirements of an ecclesiastical office in the strict sense, but which, in its specific constitution, e.g.,

---

[7] McBride, *Incardination and Excardination of Seculars*, The Catholic University of America Canon Law Studies, n. 145 (Washington, D. C.: The Catholic University of America Press, 1941), p. 430; cf. also Maroto, *Institutiones*, I, n. 582.

[8] McBride, *Incardination and Excardination of Seculars*, p. 430; Maroto, *Institutiones*, I, n. 582; Chelodi, *Ius de Personis* (2. ed., Tridenti: Libr. Edit. Tridentum, 1927), n. 132.

[9] Maroto, *Institutiones*, I, n. 579; Chelodi, *Ius de Personis*, n. 131; Wernz-Vidal, *Ius Canonicum* (7 vols. in 8, Vol. II, 2. ed., Romae: Apud Aedes Universitatis Gregorianae, 1928), II, n. 140; Cappello, *Summa Iuris Canonici*, I, 241; Vermeersch-Creusen, *Epitome Iuris Canonici* (3 vols., Vol. I, 6. ed., Mechliniae-Romae: H. Dessain, 1937), I, n. 263 (hereafter cited as *Epitome*). Thus, for example, do Vermeersch-Creusen describe this stability in the work and place just cited: "*stabile* est, stabilitate sc. *obiectiva*, ita ut . . . constituatur in Ecclesia, modo perpetuo, certus potestatis spiritualis gradus, certus iurium spiritualium complexus clerico conferendus aut semper aut quotiens adiuncta iure definita recurrunt."

[10] McBride, *op. cit.*, p. 431.

the administrator of St. Agnes' Parish, is only temporary. The law itself prescribes that it be specifically established only under certain temporary circumstances.[11]

3) Conferral (*ad normam sacrorum canonum conferendum*).—The common law prescribes the norms according to which an office is to be conferred upon an individual incumbent. The competent authority, therefore, such as a bishop, must obey these norms which the Code prescribes both for the conferral of offices in general as contained in canons 147-182, and for the conferral of particular offices, e.g., the office of vicar general.[12] It may be noted here that Maroto claimed that if a bishop were to establish *in genere* an office which does not already exist in the common law, he would nevertheless be bound to follow the prescriptions of the common law, that is, the general norms regarding conferral, when actually conferring that office in particular.[13]

4) Some participation in the power of orders or of jurisdiction (*aliquam saltem secumferens participationem ecclesiasticae potestatis sive ordinis sive iurisdictionis*).—The rather general wording of this element of the definition has given rise to controversies as to the precise meaning of the requisite ecclesiastical power, whether of orders or of jurisdiction. Some explanation or at least indication of the various opinions is therefore not out of place.

Regarding the participation in the power of orders, some authors state that this power must be one which is special and over and above that which the cleric received at ordination.[14] Other authors, on the contrary, maintain that any participation in the power already received in ordination suffices, and that consequently such functions as the celebration of Mass or the recitation of the Divine Office furnish a sufficient basis for the constituting of an office in the strict sense.[15] The writer, however, prefers an opinion which lies between these two extremes, namely, the opin-

---

[11] Canons 472-473.

[12] Cf. canons 366, § 2; 367; 424-426; 432; 434; 438; 472; 475; 1573; McBride, *Incardination and Excardination of Seculars*, pp. 433-434.
Canonici, I, 240.

[13] *Institutiones*, I, n. 579, footnote 3.

[14] Wernz-Vidal, *Ius Canonicum*, II, n. 140; Cappello, *Summa Iuris*

[15] Maroto, *Institutiones*, I, n. 579; Coronata, Institutiones, I, 240.

ion of such authors as Cocchi,[16] Claeys-Bouuaert-Simenon,[17] and McBride.[18] Thus, as McBride explains, the power of orders must be a power of orders in the strict sense. Hence the recitation of the Divine Office and other similar functions are excluded. The power of orders already acquired by ordination is nevertheless sufficient, provided "the office be of such a nature as to require the exercise of some power of orders in a given sphere, and with a view to that end bears with it a right to such exercise."[19] Such, for example, is the office of a coadjutor bishop who is given to a see (*Coadiutor Sedi datus*), for the Code itself attaches to this office the right to exercise pontifical orders, with the exception of ordinations, in the territory of the diocese.[20]

But, it must be kept in mind, not every position or office can be considered an office in the strict sense simply because it includes some power of orders already possessed in virtue of ordination. The other requirements of the definition, as contained in canon 145, § 1, must be fulfilled. Granted that there exists a public ecclesiastical position which fulfills the other requirements, but of which the sole right and obligation is limited by law to a definite sphere, such as the celebration of Mass in a particular place, then such an office must be considered as an office in the strict sense.[21]

With reference to the participation of the power of jurisdiction, whether classified as judicial or non-judicial,[22] or as legislative, judiciary, and coactive power,[23] most of the authors require ordinary power as a constitutive element for an office in the

---

[16] *Commentarium in Codicem Iuris Canonici* (8 vols. in 5, Vol. II, 4. ed., Taurinorum Augustae: Marietti, 1937), II, n. 59 (hereafter cited as *Commentarium*).

[17] *Manuale Juris Canonici ad usum Seminariorum* (3 vols., Vol. I, 3. ed., Gandae et Leodii: Seminarium Gandavense et Leodiense, 1930), I, n. 306.

[18] *Incardination and Excardination of Seculars,* p. 435 seq.

[19] McBride, *op. cit.,* p. 436.

[20] Canon 352; Lynch, *Coadjutors and Auxiliaries of Bishops,* The Catholic University of America Canon Law Studies, n. 238 (Washington, D. C.: The Catholic University of America Press, 1947), pp. 42, 59.

[21] McBride, *op. cit.,* p. 438.

[22] Canon 201, § 2.

[23] Canons 325; 2220, § 1; 2221.

strict sense.[24] For the most part they arrive at their conclusion by reason of the definition the Code gives for ordinary power of jurisdiction.[25] Other authors, however, such as Vermeersch (1858-1936)-Creusen,[26] Sipos,[27] Berutti,[28] and McBride[29] concede it is true that ordinary power cannot exist without an office in the strict sense, but they maintain that "the converse of this is not true, that an office in the strict sense cannot exist without ordinary power."[30] Accordingly Sipos contends that the competent superior could attach delegated power to an office, e.g., to the office of synodal judges, and this delegated power would be sufficient to constitute it an office in the strict sense, provided that the other requirements of the definition were present. McBride maintains that a position would fulfill the definition of an office in the strict sense provided that the common law attaches to that position "the efficacious right that some definite power be delegated to the incumbent of each specific position by the proper authorizing superior."[31] Furthermore, it can be argued from the words of the definition itself—*"aliquam saltem secumferens participationem,* etc."—that the scope of the definition is wide enough to admit the concept of delegated power.

The intention of the writer is not to attempt to solve the problem, but rather to present briefly the two opinions and their main argument. It is important juridically at least for the purpose of this work to follow one opinion or the other. Accordingly the

---

[24] Cf. Wernz-Vidal, *Ius Canonicum,* II, n. 140; Wernz, *Ius Decretalium,* II, n. 240; Chelodi, *Ius de Personis,* n. 131; Coronata, *Institutiones,* I, 332; Cappello, *Summa Iuris Canonici,* I, 241; Maroto, *Institutiones,* I, n. 579; De Meester, *Compendium,* I, 281; Bouscaren-Ellis, *Canon Law, A Text and Commentary* (Milwaukee; Bruce, 1946), 122; McDevitt, *The Renunciation of an Ecclesiastical Office,* 6.

[25] "Potestas iurisdictionis ordinaria ea est quae ipso iure adnexa est officio" —can. 197, § 1.

[26] *Epitome,* II, n. 742.

[27] *Enchiridion Iuris Canonici,* p. 127; "Ad officium sacrum an requiratur potestas ordinaria?"—*Jus Pontificium* (Romae, 1921-1940), XVI (1936), 67.

[28] *Institutiones Iuris Canonici* (6 vols., Vol. II, Pars I, Taurini Romae: Marietti, 1943), II, 139.

[29] McBride, *Incardination and Excardination of Seculars,* p. 466.

[30] McBride, *op. cit.,* p. 445.

[31] McBride, *op. cit.,* p. 446.

writer favors the opinion which requires an ordinary power of jurisdiction for the constituting of an office in the strict sense, for this opinion, it seems, is more in accord with the concept of ordinary and delegated power.

SECTION II. THE NOTION OF REMOVAL FROM OFFICE

The exact notion of the simple removal from office can best be gained through a brief consideration of the various types of removal from office as mentioned in the Code of Canon Law.

The Code, in canon 183, § 1, indicates various ways in which an ecclesiastical office may be lost, that is, by renunciation, by privation, by removal, by transfer, and by the lapse of the previously defined duration of time.[32] While it is true that the Code makes a distinction in this canon between *privatio* and *amotio,* still in canon 192, where the question of privation or removal is considered, no such distinction appears from the wording of the canon, but the very general word *privatio* is used. Suffice it to explain here that the word *privatio,* as used in canon 192, is a general term which includes any type of removal from office.[33]

Privation or removal from office in general may be defined as an act by which a cleric is dispossessed of his office.[34] The Code itself gives the origin or source whence the act of removal has its rise. A removal is incurred either automatically by force of the law (*ipso iure*), or in view of a legitimate superior's action in a given case (ex facto legitimi Superioris), i.e., *ab homine.*[35]

---

[32] "Amittitur officium ecclesiasticum renuntiatione, privatione, amotione, translatione, lapsu temporis praefiniti." Concerning the renunciation of an office the reader is referred to the dissertation already mentioned—*The Renunciation of an Ecclesiastical Office*—by McDevitt. Concerning the removal of pastors by means of the administrative process cf. Connor—*The Administrative Removal of Pastors,* and Meier, *Penal Administrative Procedure Against Negligent Pastors,* The Catholic University of America Canon Law Studies, n. 140 (Washington, D. C.: The Catholic University of America Press, 1941).

[33] Chelodi, *Ius de Personis,* n. 149, p. 252, footnote n. 1.

[34] Maroto, *Institutiones Iuris Canonici,* I, n. 685. Cf. also Coronata, *Institutiones,* I, 321; Wernz-Vidal, *Ius Canonicum,* II, n. 360; ". . . ablatio officii ecclesiastici a clerico legitime obtenti."—Sipos, *Enchiridion Iuris Canonici,* p. 149; Beste, *Introductio in Codicem,* p. 211.

[35] Canon 192, § 1.

Privation or removal which is incurred *ipso facto* follows as an automatic effect of the law upon the commission of an act or misdeed to which the law itself attaches the penalty of privation. Such a removal is inflicted by the law itself without any intervention of a superior. It is expedient sometimes that the competent superior give a simple declaratory sentence in order to specify the fact which brought about the privation. But the ordinary cannot in public cases remit the penalty or substitute for it some other means of correction.[36]

Instances wherein an *ipso facto* resulting privation is incurred are found in the Fifth Book of Code, as also in the cases of tacit renunciation enumerated in canon 188, for the latter must be regarded as instances in which the operation of the law itself brings about the privation of office.[37] It is important to keep in mind that such a removal is properly designated as a *privatio* in the strict sense, for it presupposes a delict and is inflicted as a vindictive penalty.[38]

Before specific consideration is given to each of the types of removal effected *ab homine,* it is important to point out a distinction between offices which has a direct bearing on the type of removal to be inflicted. Offices are divided by reason of the time for which they are conferred into those whose incumbents are irremovable, and into those whose incumbents are removable. This terminology has been adapted from the divisions proper to benefices.[39] Accordingly the former offices are those which are conferred perpetually —*"in perpetuum"*; the latter offices, also called manual or temporary offices, are those which are conferred revocably—*"revocabiliter."*

By reason of the manner in which a privation is inflicted or a removal decreed by the act of the ordinary or of the legitimate superior, one may contemplate three possible types. These reflect either a judicial, or an administrative, or a simple character.

---

[36] Canons 2237, § 1, n. 3; 1948, 2°; Bęste, *op. cit.*, p. 211.

[37] Cf. canons 2266, 2396-2398.

[38] "Privatio, sensu proprio, sine culpa non intelligitur, cum sit gravissima sanctio vindicativa; incurritur autem aut ipso iure aut sententia iudicis"—Chelodi, *Ius de Personis,* n. 149; Beste, *loc. cit.*

[39] Canon 1411, 4°.

a—Judicial privation is that which is imposed according to the rules of a strict judicial trial, as outlined in canons 1933-1959, upon the incumbent of an ecclesiastical office.[40] It is, like the *ipso iure* effected removal, a *privatio* in the strict sense. It has the nature of a vindictive penalty, and always supposes a delict—and that indeed a delict which is expressed in the law as meriting such a penalty.[41] The causes for which such a privation should, or at least can, be inflicted may be found in the alphabetical index of the Code under the word *"privatio."* It would be beyond the purpose of this work to list these causes at this point. However, it may well be noted here that, if there is question of the privation of an incumbent from an irremovable office which also is a benefice, then a collegiate tribunal of three judges is necessary, whereas in the judicial privation of an incumbent from his removable benefice a trial by one judge is sufficient.[42]

b—Administrative privation or removal, which is also called economic or disciplinary removal, is that which is applied by means of an administrative process.[43] It was instituted precisely for the good of souls, and since it does not essentially presuppose guilt, it is not necessarily intended as a punishment. It is a special process which abstracts from the observance of the strictly judicial solemnities. Its forthright purpose is to make provision for the well-being of the parish through the removal of its pastor in circumstances which insinuate a demand for his removal.[44]

The Code recounts the formalities which must be followed in the administrative removal of both irremovable and removable pastors.[45] So, though such a removal does not involve any strictly judicial action, it definitely calls for the use of a special process as regulated by the law itself.

---

[40] Coronata, *Institutiones,* I, 322; Beste, *op. cit.,* p. 211; Meier, *Penal Administrative Procedure Against Negligent Pastors,* p. 92.

[41] Cf. canons 2286; 2298, 6°; 2299.

[42] Canon 1576; Beste, *op. cit.,* pp. 211-212.

[43] Connor, *The Administrative Removal of Pastors,* p. 3.

[44] Connor, *op. cit.,* pp. 2-5.

[45] *Lib. IV, Titulus XXVII, de modo procedendi in remotione parochorum inamovibilium*—canons 2147-2156; *Titulus XXVIII, de modo procedendi in remotione parochorum amovibilium*—canons 2157-2161.

While it is true also that this type of removal is not intended primarily as a punishment, nevertheless there is a type of administrative removal which is definitely penal in character. Such, for example, is the penal administrative privation which is inflicted upon a pastor as punishment for the criminal deeds exhaustively enumerated in canons 2182 and 2382. This removal, which is also called a processual privation for the sake of distinguishing it from a strictly judicial privation, is indeed a privation in the strict sense, even though it be inflicted in an administrative manner.[46] Also penal in nature are the processes delineated in the Fourth Book of the Code under Titles XXX, XXXI, and XXXIII. Administrative removal, though it always connotes an administrative process, may therefore be either non-penal or penal in character. In either assumption the basic reason for action on the part of the superior is the salvation of souls, and not the punishment of a guilty cleric.[47]

c—Simple privation or removal, also called by the authors a revocation, a dismissal, a discretional dislodgment from office, or a precautionary dispossession of office, with a view to distinguishing it from the two types of privation or removal just treated, is the type of removal with which this work is precisely concerned.[48] It is necessary here but to indicate the essential elements of this type of removal, for their fuller explanation will evolve in the course of the following chapters. Simple removal is concerned first

[46] Wernz-Vidal, *Ius Canonicum,* II, n. 361; Connor, *The Administrative Removal of Pastors,* p. 4; Meier, *Penal Administrative Procedure Against Negligent Pastors,* p. 93.

[47] Meier, *op. cit.,* p. 90.

[48] Cappello, *Summa Iuris Canonici,* I, 267: "Dicitur *privatio,* si officium aufertur in poenam; *amotio,* si potissimum ob causam boni publici, sive clericus sit reus sive etiam innocens; *dimissio,* si agitur de munere quod fuit ad nutum concessum"; Beste, *Introductio in Codicem,* p. 211: "Ratione processus in eius applicatione servandi, haec [privatio ferendae sententiae seu ab homine] erit . . . arbitraria seu ad nutum superioris, si, nulla servata processus forma, ductu dumtaxat principiorum naturalis aequitatis pronuntietur. Privatio iudicialis etiam specifice appellatur privatio; oeconomica, remotio seu amotio; arbitraria, revocatio vel amotio." Ayrinhac (General Legislation in the New Code of Canon Law [New York: Benziger & Co., 1923], p. 351) describes the simple removal which is unattended with any process as an "informal" privation.

of all with removable incumbents of office, as canon 192, § 3, clearly indicates. But this type of removal cannot be used by the ordinary if there is question of removing removable pastors, i.e., such pastors whose removal is regulated by the norms for administrative removal.

Simple removal furthermore may be decreed by the ordinary for any just cause according to his prudent judgment, even though there is no offense on the part of the cleric. While no certain form of procedure is required for such an act of removal, still the ordinary or competent superior is bound to have a just cause and to observe natural equity when depriving a cleric of his office. The deprivation itself has no effect until notice of it has been communicated by the superior to the cleric in question. Finally, against such an act of removal the one removed may seek recourse *"in devolutivo"* with the Apostolic See.

CHAPTER IV

The Competent Superior for the Act of Simple Removal From Office

Before any specific treatment is given to the various offices whose incumbents are subject to the act of simple removal from office, there is need of determining who is the competent ecclesiastical authority to decree such a removal from office. The Code itself clearly states that simple removal can be decreed by the ordinary.[1]

Hence it must be determined who are included under the term "ordinary" in this matter. According to the Code, the following persons, unless an express exception is made, are included under the term *Ordinarius*: The Roman Pontiff for the entire Church, and for their respective territories residential bishops, abbots and prelates *nullius,* and their vicars general, administrators, vicars and prefects apostolic, and all those who, by the provisions of the law or of approved constitutions, succeed during the vacancy the aforementioned ordinaries in the rule of their territory; finally, for their subjects, the major superiors of exempt clerical religious institutes.[2]

With regard to the question of simple removal, who among these ordinaries has the right or the power to decree the removal of a cleric from an ecclesiastical office? It is evident that residential bishops have this right over the removable incumbents of office in their territory. Moreover, since the act of removal from office is not an act of orders but an act of voluntary jurisdiction, the bishop can exercise this right even though he is outside his diocese, and even if he has not yet been consecrated, provided only that he has taken canonical possession of his see.[3] Likewise, vicars and prefects apostolic,[4] and also abbots and prelates *nullius,*[5] have the

[1] Canon 192, § 3: ". . . privatio decerni ab Ordinario potest."

[2] Canon 198, § 1.

[3] Canons 201, § 3; 334, §§ 2, 3; Beste, *Introductio in Codicem,* p. 200.

[4] Canon 294, § 1.

[5] Canon 323, § 1.

rights of a residential bishop in their respective territories, and are competent in this matter without question. So, too, permanent apostolic administrators[6] and coadjutor bishops who are given to a totally incapacitated bishop[7] enjoy the same rights as a residential bishop, and therefore are competent.

However, concerning the other ordinaries—aside from the major superiors of exempt clerical religious institutes—included under the term *Ordinarius,* some further explanation is necessary to ascertain whether they, such as the vicar general, or the vicar capitular (or diocesan administrator), are competent in the matter of effecting a simple removal from office.

It seems that the vicar general can remove the removable incumbents of office in the diocese. First of all, by virtue of his office the vicar general enjoys the same ordinary jurisdiction as the bishop in spiritual and temporal matters, except with regard to such matters as the bishop has reserved to himself, or with regard to which by law there is need of a special mandate from the bishop.[8]

The law does deny to the vicar general the right to bestow benefices[9] or to grant ecclesiastical offices[10] if he does not have a special mandate, except when the see is impeded through the absence of the bishop by captivity, banishment, or exile, or by his inability to fulfill the duties of his office, so that it is impossible for him to communicate with his diocese.[11] In such circumstances the vicar general certainly would be competent to institute the removal from office, for he then enjoys the full ordinary power of the bishop. Aside from these circumstances the vicar general is further restricted by the law in that he cannot transfer a cleric from an office, since a transfer implies not only the loss of an office but also the bestowal of another in place of the one given up by the cleric.[12] It seems clear, too, that the vicar general cannot decree a removal

---

[6] Canon 315, § 1.

[7] Canon 351, § 2.

[8] Canon 368, § 1.

[9] Canon 1432, § 2.

[10] Canon 152.

[11] Canon 429, § 1.

[12] Canon 193, § 1; Galvin, *The Administrative Transfer of Pastors,* p. 115.

from office as a penalty, unless he has a special mandate or unless the see is impeded in the way just described.[13]

But more closely related to the present work are the observations of Connor regarding the power of the vicar general to institute the process of the administrative removal of pastors. The author concludes that since the Code does not require a special mandate in order that the vicar general may institute removal proceedings, he may, in virtue of his office, administratively remove a pastor, provided that the bishop has not generally or in a particular case withdrawn jurisdiction in this matter.[14] Connor rejects the arguments of those who hold the opposite opinion by raising the question: "Why should the legislator enumerate several cases in which the vicar general requires a special mandate, unless he intends that the list should be exhaustive?" But the Code does not expressly state anywhere that the vicar general needs a special mandate to remove pastors.

The same teaching, it seems, can be applied to the question of simple removal with but one exception as made by the Code. That exception is that the vicar general cannot without a special mandate remove parochial vicars, that is, the vicar oeconome (or administrator) of a vacant parish, the vicar substitute for a pastor absent from his parish beyond a week, the vicar adjutant who supplies for an incapacitated pastor, and finally the vicars known as assistants.[15] Since no other exception to simple removal on the part of the vicar general is contained in the law itself, the writer believes it safe to conclude that the vicar general can decree a simple removal as far as the other removable incumbents of offices are concerned, unless the bishop has reserved this to himself. However, from the practical viewpoint, he would rarely if ever use such a power, especially since he could neither grant the one removed from office a new office, nor appoint a new incumbent to the vacant office without a special mandate. Moreover, he must always keep in mind the prescription of the Code that he take care not to use his power contrary to the good pleasure of the bishop.[16] Hence

---

[13] Canon 2220, § 2; cf. also canon 429, § 1.

[14] Connor, *The Administrative Removal of Pastors,* p. 82.

[15] Cf. canons 477, § 1; 472-476.

[16] Canon 369, § 2.

prudence demands that the vicar general consult the bishop once and for all to determine exactly what powers he can exercise with regard to the question of simple removal from office.

The same arguments and conclusions, it seems, may be made about the vicar delegate who is appointed by a vicar or a prefect apostolic, and who enjoys the same jurisdiction as does the vicar general of a bishop.[17] In practice this vicar delegate will probably be identical with the pro-vicar or pro-prefect whom the Code requires to be appointed by the vicar or the prefect apostolic upon his succession to office.[18] Should they be two distinct officials, however, then the pro-vicar or pro-prefect enjoys only that power which is delegated to him by the prefect apostolic.[19] But if the see should become vacant or impeded, as indicated in canon 309, § 2,[20] then the pro-vicar or pro-prefect would have the right to decree removals.

It may happen however that the bishop has, in the event he is prevented from ruling his see, delegated some other ecclesiastical person to rule the diocese. This person could, depending on the extent of the powers delegated to him, have the power to confer offices and remove the incumbents of the same. On the other hand, the Holy See may have chosen the one who is to rule the see when these extraordinary conditions exist, and he too, unless restricted by the mandate of the Holy See, would be fully competent in the question of removal.[21]

In the event that the government of the see is taken over by the cathedral chapter (or by the diocesan consultors as is the rule in this country), either under the circumstances mentioned in canon 429, § 3,[22] or when the see is vacant as is stated in canons 430,

[17] S.C. de Prop. Fide., litt., 8 dec. 1919—*AAS* (1920), 120; Bouscaren, *The Canon Law Digest* (2 vols., Milwaukee: Bruce, 1934-1943), I, 144.

[18] Canon 309, § 1.

[19] Canon 309, § 2.

[20] "Pro-vicarius aut Pro-praefectus nullam habet, vivente Vicario aut Praefecto, potestatem, nisi quae fuerit ab eodem sibi commissa; sed deficiente Vicario aut Praefecto, vel eorum iurisdictione impedita ad norman can. 429, § 1, totum debet regimen assumere et in hoc munere permanere, donec a Sancta Sede aliter fuerit provisum."

[21] Canon 429, § 1.

[22] "His deficientibus, vel, uti supra dictum est, impeditis, Capitulum ecclesiae cathedralis suum Vicarium constituat, qui regimen assumat cum potestate Vicarii Capitularis."

§ 1 and 431, § 1,[23] then the vicar capitular (the diocesan administrator in the United States), elected by the chapter (or by the diocesan consultors), is to govern the diocese according to the norms of law.[24]

The question then is: Does the vicar capitular or diocesan administrator have the right to remove the removable incumbents of offices? The Code clearly states that the vicar capitular (or diocesan administrator), has, once he is deputed by the chapter (or by the diocesan consultors), the ordinary jurisdiction of the bishop in temporal and spiritual affairs, except in matters wherein his jurisdiction is expressly denied by the law.[25] The only restrictions put upon the vicar capitular or the diocesan administrator as such in so far as the act of simple removal from office is concerned, that is, aside from the general prescription that he is forbidden to do anything prejudicial to the diocese or to the episcopal rights,[26] may be found in the regulations of the Code concerning the removal of the chancellor, the vice-chancellors and notaries, the *officialis* and the *vice-officialis,* the defender of the bond, and the promoter of justice.[27] Accordingly the chancellor, the vice-chancellors and the notaries cannot be removed by the vicar capitular or the diocesan administrator except with the consent of the chapter or the board of consultors.[28] Moreover, in virtue of canon 105, 1° any attempt by the vicar capitular or the diocesan administrator at the act of removal without the consent of the cathedral chapter or the diocesan consultors would be invalid.[29]

[23] Canon 430, § 1: "Sedes episcopalis vacat Episcopi morte, renuntiatione a Romano Pontifice acceptata, translatione ac privatione Episcopo intimata"; canon 431, § 1: "Sede vacante, nisi adfuerit Administrator Apostolicus vel aliter a Sancta Sede provisum fuerit, ad Capitulum ecclesiae cathedralis regimen dioecesis devolvitur."

[24] Canon 432, § 2: "Capitulum ecclesiae cathedralis, sede vacante, . . . debet Vicarium Capitularem qui loco sui dioecesim regat . . . constituere." Cf. also canons 423-428.

[25] Canon 435, §§ 1, 2; cf. also canon 427 regarding diocesan consultors.

[26] Canon 435, § 3.

[27] The writer prescinds at this point from any discussion as to whether these offices are ecclesiastical offices in the strict sense. This matter will be considered below in the next chapter.

[28] Canon 373, § 5: ". . . non autem a Vicario Capitulari [removeri possunt], nisi de consensu Capituli."

[29] Canon 105, 1°: "Si consensus exigatur, Superior contra earundem votum invalide agit."

The *officialis* and *vice-officialis,* on the other hand, cannot be removed from office by the vicar capitular or the diocesan administrator except for a crime for which they have been convicted through a judicial procedure.[30] The same limitation applies with reference to the incumbents of the offices of defender of the bond and of promoter of justice.[31]

It seems logical to conclude therefore that the vicar capitular or the diocesan administrator is competent with regard to the act of effecting a simple removal from office, provided that the above mentioned restrictions are kept in mind as well as any other limitations which the Code puts on the removal power of all ordinaries and those who rule in their stead, for example, the removal of synodal examiners and parish priest consultors, in which instance the law requires a grave cause and the consultation of the cathedral chapter or of the diocesan consultors.[32]

In addition to the ordinaries already considered, the term *Ordinarius,* as indicated above,[33] includes the major superiors of exempt clerical religious institutes, that is, the abbot primate, the abbot superior of a monastic congregation, the abbots of independent monasteries, though these belong to some monastic congregation, the supreme head of any religious institute, the provincial superiors, the vicars of all the aforesaid, and such others as have authority in the same fashion as have these vicars.[34]

That these superiors are competent to decree the simple removal from office of their subjects is evident not only from the fact that in being ordinaries they are comprehended in the wording of canon 192, § 3, but also from the explicit regulations in the Code which pertain to the removal of religious from particular offices. So it is that pastors who belong to religious communities are removable *ad nutum,* both at the will of the local ordinary notifying the religious superior, and also at the will of the respective religious

---

[30] Canon 1573, § 5: Dugan, *The Judiciary Department* of *The Diocesan Curia,* The Catholic University of America Canon Law Studies, n. 26 (Washington, D. C.: The Catholic University of America, 1925), p. 40.

[31] Canon 1590, § 1.

[32] Canon 388; cf. also canon 1574, § 2.

[33] Cf. *supra,* p. 46.

[34] Canons 198, § 1; 488, 8°.

superior, notifying the local ordinary. Both have equal rights in this matter, so that neither of them needs the previous consent of the other.[85] The same regulation applies with reference to the removal of the parochial vicar who exercises the actual care of souls in a parish united in full right (*pleno iure*) to a religious house, to a capitular church, or to any other legal person, provided this vicar is a member of a religious institute,[86] of the other parochial vicars dealt with in canons 472-476,[87] and of the rector of a church who is a religious.[88]

Generally the religious superiors will follow the norms of the common law in their decrees of simple removal, that is, those norms which are contained in the general rule of canon 192, § 3, and in the prescriptions of other particular canons which relate to specific offices. However, the question of removal from office may be determined more precisely by the constitutions of each religious institute. The superiors then are bound to follow the special law of their institute in addition to the requirements of the common law.[89]

Examples of such particular legislation pertaining to the act of the simple removal from office as exercisable by the competent authority are:

a) in the Order of Friars Minor, with regard to a local superior such as the Guardian, who indeed is of a truly prelatial rank in that he enjoys in the external forum an exercise of jurisdiction as limited according to the norm of the constitutions of the Order, the Constitutions indicate that if the common good or any other

[85] Canon 454, § 5: "Parochi autem, ad religiosam familiam pertinentes, sunt semper, ratione personae, amovibiles ad nutum tam loci Ordinarii, monito Superiore, quam Superioris, monito Ordinario, aequo iure, non requisito alterius consensu . . ."; cf. also canon 631, §§ 1, 3.

[86] Canon 471, § 3: "Vicarius si sit religiosus, est amovibilis sicut parochus religiosus de quo in can. 454, § 5. . . ."

[87] Canon 477, § 1: "Vicarii paroeciales de quibus in can. 472-476, si religiosi sint, amoveri possunt ad normam can. 454, § 5. . . ."

[88] Canon 486: ". . . quod si rector fuerit religiosus, servetur, circa eius remotionem, praescriptum can. 454, § 5."

[89] Schaefer, *De Religiosis ad Normam Codicis Iuris Canonici* (3. ed., Romae: Typis Polyglottis Vaticanis, 1940), p. 343 (hereafter cited as *De Religiosis*); Coronata, *Institutiones Iuris Canonici,* I, 324; Berutti, *Institutiones Iuris Canonici,* II, 300, footnote n. 1.

truly grave cause demands his removal, "the Minister Provincial with the consent of his Definitorium may decide these things outside the Chapter."[40] Pastors too are removed by the "Minister Provincial with the consent of the Definitorium . . . other necessary things being observed."[41] The phrase "other necessary things being observed" no doubt refers to the fact that the local ordinary is to be notified of such a removal.[42] It very likely contemplates also the required presence of a just cause, and the observance of natural equity.[43]

b) In the Dominican Order, with regard to the Provincial Vicar, the Constitutions regulate that the Provincial may, even alone, appoint a Vicar either over the whole province or over any part of the province, and he may also for good and just cause remove him from office at will.[44] If there is question of removing a conventual Prior, this matter is to be taken up by the Council of the province.[45] Concerning the removal of pastors, however, the Constitutions merely repeat the Code legislation.[46]

It is clear therefore that religious superiors who are ordinaries are competent in the matter of effecting a simple removal from office. But—the question may be asked—do local religious superiors who are not ordinaries, but who nevertheless are true superiors, have the power to decree a removal from office? Canon 192, § 3, seems indeed to indicate that such power belongs only to ordinaries. Yet in canon 454, § 5, which is concerned precisely with the re-

[40] *The Rule and General Constitutions of the Friars Minor* (Paterson, New Jersey: St. Anthony Guild Press, 1936), n. 574. Schaefer (*op. cit.*, p. 235) explains that the term *Definitorium* is synonymous with Council (Consilium): "Consilium (Definitorium, Discretorium, in can. 655, § 1, etiam Capitulum nominatum) est coetus a iure communi vel a Constitutionibus ordinatus, ut Superiores in designatis imprimis gravioribus negotiis adiuvent et auxilium afferant"; cf. also canons 516, § 1; 105 1°.

[41] *The Rule and General Constitutions of the Friars Minor,* p. 148, n. 687; cf. canon 105, 1°.

[42] Canon 454, § 5.

[43] Canon 192, § 3.

[44] *Constitutiones Fratrum Sacri Ordinis Praedicatorum Inchoatae in Capitulo Generali Provincialium Romae celebrato a. 1924* (Romae: Ex Typographia R. Garroni, 1925), n. 588.

[45] *Op. cit.*, p. 137, n. 605, j.

[46] Canon 454, § 5.

moval of pastors who belong to a religious community, the general term *"Superior"* is used in designation of the competent authority who enjoys this right equally with the local ordinary.

Under the term *"Superior"* in the law are included, even in the strict sense, all those who *ex officio* exercise ordinary religious power, whether jurisdictional or dominative, over a house, a province, or the institute itself.[47] Moreover those superiors, if they belong to an exempt clerical institute, have according to the constitutions and the common law ecclesiastical jurisdiction for the internal as well as the external forum.[48] Since canon 454, § 5, contains no note of specification as to which superior is competent, it could include the local superior.[49] Hence, as Clancy maintains, it seems logical to conclude that the Code leaves the determination of the competent superior to the constitutions (*ad normam constitutionum*).[50]

If, then, the local superior is given authority in the constitutions of his institute to present the religious who is to exercise the office of pastor or parochial vicar,[51] he may also remove such a pastor or vicar, and thereupon inform the local ordinary of what has been done.[52] Whether the local superior can remove any of the parochial vicars mentioned in canons 471-476 will depend again on whether or not he is declared competent in the constitutions or in other particular laws of his institute. Clancy maintains that if the local superior is permitted to appoint these vicars, he in all probability will be given the power to remove them.[53] He will then be bound, in the opinion of the present writer, to observe the requirements of canon 192, § 3, that is, he must have a just cause and observe the demands of natural equity, as well as whatever particular requirements the constitutions may make in this regard.

---

[47] Schaefer, *De Religiosis,* p. 215.

[48] Canon 501, § 1.

[49] Schaefer, *op. cit.,* p. 217.

[50] Clancy, *The Local Religious Superior,* The Catholic University of America Canon Law Studies, n. 175 (Washington, D. C.: The Catholic University of America Press, 1943), p. 28.

[51] Cf. canons 456; 471, § 3; 454, § 5.

[52] Clancy, *op. cit.,* p. 109.

[53] *Op. cit.,* p. 111, footnote n. 245.

CHAPTER V

Incumbents in Office Who Are Subject to the Act of Simple Removal

Once it has been established who is the competent ecclesiastical superior to decree the simple removal from office, it remains to determine the incumbents in office who are subject to this type of removal which entails no need of any process, but which, as far as the general principle enunciated in canon 192, § 3, is concerned, is decreed simply with an act of the legitimate superior. The canon itself simply states that the ordinary can decree this removal from all offices whose incumbents are removable, with the exception of the pastoral office inasfar as the removal of its incumbents is regulated by a special administrative process.[1]

As far as the words of canon 192, § 3, are concerned, there is no indication as to whether all ecclesiastical offices, even those which are such in only the wide sense, are to be governed by the principles of this canon when there is question of the removal of incumbents from them, or whether the application of these principles is restricted to the removal of incumbents from ecclesiastical offices in the strict sense alone.[2] But, to repeat for the sake of emphasis and clarity what was pointed out in a preceding chapter,[3] canon 145, § 2, states that in the law the mention of ecclesiastical office is to be taken in the strict sense, unless the contrary is clear from the context. Since the context of canon 192 contains no such contrary indication, it seems clear that *juridically* only ecclesiastical offices in the strict sense come under the principles therein enunciated.

Inasmuch as the present writer favors the opinion which, with

---

[1] Canon 192, § 3: "Si de amovibili, privatio decerni potest ab Ordinario . . . sed certum procedendi modum sequi minime tenetur, salvo canonum praescripto circa paroecias amovibiles. . . ." Cf. also canons 2157-2161.

[2] Cf. *supra*, p. 35, where the distinction between offices in the strict and wide sense is explained.

[3] Cf. *supra, loc. cit.*

reference to the jurisdictional content of an office, postulates for every office in the strict sense that it contain a jurisdiction which is of an ordinary, and not merely of a delegated character, some consideration must be given to the determination of what principle is to govern the removal of incumbents from the other offices which are such in only a wide sense, and consequently do not connote the possession of an ordinary power of jurisdiction. Accordingly the present chapter will be divided into two sections: the one to show which offices in the matter of the removal of their incumbents juridically come under the principles of canon 192, § 3; the other to apply by analogy the same principles to the removal of incumbents from the offices which can be so designated in only a wide sense. In each section attention will be given to the specific regulations made by the Code with regard to the removal of incumbents from particular offices, that is, those regulations which must be observed in addition to the general norm of canon 192, § 3.

SECTION I. INCUMBENTS JURIDICALLY SUBJECT TO THE PROVISIONS OF CANON 192, § 3

Article I. The Vicar General

The position of a vicar general is undoubtedly an ecclesiastical office in the strict sense. It meets the requirements for such an office as indicated in canon 145, § 1, and from the common law derives its content of an ordinary power of jurisdiction which can be exercised in the external and the internal forum alike.[4] It is likewise clear from the Code that the bishop may remove the vicar general *ad nutum,*[5] or by means of an act of simple revocation.[6]

But it must be clearly understood, both for this office and for all offices whose incumbents are removable *ad nutum,* that such an act of removal is not admissible as an arbitrary affair or as a matter of caprice or whim. While it is true that the question in the last analysis is left to the discretion or prudent judgment of the ordinary, still the requirements of canon 192, § 3, must be

[4] Canon 366, § 1: "... constituendus est ab Episcopo Vicarius Generalis, qui ipsum potestate ordinaria in toto territorio adiuvet."

[5] Canon 366, § 2.

[6] Canon 371.

observed, even when a removal is made *ad nutum*. In other words, there must be at hand a just cause in the prudent estimation of the bishop, and natural equity must be observed. This is the teaching of most of the authors.[7]

Among these authors some, such as Vidal (1868-1939),[8] Chelodi, (1880-1922)[9] and Coronata,[10] emphasize that special care is to be taken in the matter of safeguarding the good name or reputation of the vicar general if he is removed aside from any guilt on his part, otherwise the vicar can have recourse to the Holy See to save his honor. Sipos demands even a grave cause for the removal.[11]

It seems clear also from the teachings of the authors that the presence of a just or reasonable cause is required, not for the validity of the bishop's act of removal, but for its lawfulness only.[12] Finally, even though the bishop must have a cause for decreeing the removal, he is not bound to reveal that cause to the vicar general who is being removed.[13]

Thus the present writer does not agree at all with Augustine, who maintains that the removal which can permissibly be made *ad nutum* may be decreed with or without reason.[14] The expression *amotio ad nutum,* so it seems logical to conclude, is in practice

---

[7] Cf. Cappello, *Summa Iuris Canonici,* I, 350; Vermeersch-Creusen, *Epitome,* I, n. 483; Chelodi, *Ius de Personis,* n. 200.

[8] *Ius Canonicum,* II, n. 637.

[9] *Loc. cit.*

[10] *Institutiones,* I. 502, footnote n. 6: ". . . est enim officium *ad nutum* amovibile; *ad nutum* autem non de quolibet arbitrio, sed de arbitrio rationabili intelligendum est; contra laesionem honoris quae forte ex revocatione sequatur patet recursus ad S. Sedem."

[11] *Enchiridion Iuris Canonici,* p. 260.

[12] Cf. e.g., the teaching of Coronata (*loc. cit.*), which he bases on Wernz, *Ius Decretalium,* II, tit. XXXVII, n. 806: "ut revocatio licite fiat, ratio habenda est *honoris* Vicarii Generalis, et iusta gravisque causa intercedat necesse est."—Cf. also Sipos, *loc. cit.*

[13] Blat, *Commentarium Textus Codicis Iuris Canonici* (5 vols. in 7, Romae: Ex Typographia Pontificia in Instituto Pii IX, 1921-1927, Vol. II, 2. ed., 1921), II, 396 (hereafter cited as *Commentarium*).

[14] Augustine, *A Commentary on the New Code of Canon Law* (8 vols., St. Louis: Herder & Co., 1925-1938, Vol. II, 6. ed., 1936; Vol. VII, 3. ed., 1930), II, 396, 408 (hereafter cited as *A Commentary on Canon Law*).

synonymous with the concept of revocation or of simple removal, and signifies primarily that no process whatsoever is needed for the effecting of such a removal, not even the consent or advice of others. Though a grave cause would not always be necessary in order that the ordinary may remove the incumbents of offices who are removable *ad nutum,* still some just or reasonable cause is required, and equity must be observed.

Article II. The Diocesan Chancellor

In order to determine whether the office of diocesan chancellor is an office in the strict sense, consideration must be given to the exact connotation of the term "jurisdiction." McBride[15] has questioned this office on the grounds that the incumbent does not participate in the power of jurisdiction. However, in ecclesiastical law the term "jurisdiction" refers to whatever essential element pertains to the power of ruling, whether that power exists as a legislative, as an executive and administrative, or as a judicial and interpretative function.[16]

Moreover, the Code itself employs the term in this extensive sense through the use of the term *"regimen"* as a synonym for jurisdiction.[17]

On the basis of this argumentation Prince maintains that the office of chancellor can be said at least in some degree to participate in this fulness of the power of jurisdiction.[18] The author argues that the duties which the law attaches to the office of the chancellor, namely, the care and especially the legal authentication of jurisdictional documents, are a necessary part of the ordinary's exercise of jurisdictional power. Coronata appears to agree with this argumentation. For he holds that the chancellor's office is truly an ecclesiastical office, but that the same cannot be said of

---

[15] *Incardination and Excardination of Seculars,* p. 463.

[16] Prümmer, *Manuale Iuris Canonici in Usum Scholarum* (3. ed., Friburgi Brisgoviae, 1922), p. 119.

[17] Canon 196; cf. Roberti, *De Processibus* (2 vols., Vol. I, 2. ed., Romae: Apud Custodiam Librariam Pontificii Instituti Utriusque Iuris, 1941), I, n. 38.

[18] *The Diocesan Chancellor,* The Catholic University of America Canon Law Studies, n. 167 (Washington, D. C.: The Catholic University of America Press, 1942), p. 45.

the office of other notaries.[19] Maroto[20] and Manning[21] similarly agree that the position of chancellor is an office in the strict sense.

The chancellor can be removed from office or suspended from its exercise by the person who appointed him to the office, or also by his successor or superior, but not by the vicar capitular or the diocesan administrator without the consent of the cathedral chapter or of the diocesan consultors.[22] Since the Code directs that the chancellor be appointed by the bishop,[23] it seems that normally the vicar general lacks competence for removing him from office. However, if the bishop has given a special mandate to his vicar general for constituting a priest in the office of chancellor, it seems that then the vicar general could remove the chancellor in consequence of the fact that he himself had legally appointed him. Prince maintains that the vicar general would act validly in such a case even without a special mandate for the removal.[24]

Regardless of which superior decrees the removal, there must exist a just reason and due regard for natural equity in the particular circumstances. An appointment to some other office must be made, if possible, in order to care for the priest who has been removed from his office, and, what is more important, the removal must be made in such a manner that it does not appear like a penalty when there has been no delict.[25]

Article III. The Officialis and Vice-Officialis

The position of *officialis* in a diocese also fulfills all the requirements of an ecclesiastical office in the strict sense. Constituted in

[19] *Institutiones,* I, 504. It must be remembered that Coronata holds to the opinion that an ecclesiastical office in the strict sense carries with it an ordinary power of jurisdiction. Cf. *op. cit.,* I, 332.

[20] *Institutiones,* I, n. 742.

[21] *The Free Conferral of Offices,* The Catholic University of America Canon Law Studies, n. 219 (Washington, D. C.: The Catholic University of America Press, 1945), p. 24.

[22] Canon 373, § 5: "Omnes possunt removeri aut suspendi ab eo qui illos constituit aut ab eius successore aut Superiore, non autem a Vicario Capitulari, nisi de consensu Capituli."

[23] Canon 372, § 1.

[24] *The Diocesan Chancellor,* p. 54.

[25] *Op. cit.,* p. 57.

a generic manner by the common law, it derives from that same law a definite judicial power of jurisdiction attached to it, which power is therefore ordinary.[26]

Some dispute exists, however, with regard to the position of *vice-officialis,* since the authors differ as to whether it has ordinary power attached to it.[27] Roberti maintains that all *vice-officiales* come under the name of *officialis,* and whatever is done by each is understood as done by the *officialis.*[28] Cappello holds that the power of the *vice-officialis* is beyond doubt an ordinary power, since by the very fact that he is selected by the bishop as *vice-officialis* he derives his power from the common law itself apart from any special act of delegation on the part of the bishop.[29] Dugan[30] seems to agree with this opinion, which, as he points out, has a clear basis in canon 1577, § 2,[31] and canon 1578.[32] Moreover the qualifications are the same for both the *officialis* and *vice-officialis.*[33]

Nevertheless Coronata is of the opinion that the *vice-officiales* do not have ordinary power. They are not so he thinks, to be considered as judges delegated in solidum, but rather as assistants to the *officialis,* whose place they supply in a case of necessity.[34] Augustine agrees with that opinion.[35] Perhaps these two authors and others who agree with them are somewhat influenced in their opinion by the wording of the Code which refers to the vice-officialis as *"adiutores."*[36]

---

[26] "Quilibet Episcopus tenetur officialem eligere cum potestate ordinaria iudicandi, a Vicario Generali distinctum, nisi . . ."—canon 1573, § 1; Cappello, *Summa Iuris Canonici,* III (2. ed., 1940), Dugan, *The Judiciary Department of the Diocesan Curia,* p. 38.

[27] Cf. canon 1573, § 3.

[28] Roberti, *De Processibus,* I, n. 99.

[29] *Summa Iuris Canonici,* III, 27.

[30] *Op. cit.,* p. 38.

[31] "Eidem praeest officialis vel vice-officialis, cuius est processum diregere, et decernere quae pro iustitiae administratione in causa quae agitur necessaria sunt."

[32] ". . . Episcopus semper potest trubunali ipse per se praeesse; sed valde expedit ut causas . . . iudicandas relinquat tribunali ordinario, cui praesit officialis vel vice-officialis."

[33] Canon 1573, § 4.

[34] *Institutiones,* III, 26.

[35] *A Commentary on Canon Law,* VII, 31.

[36] Canon 1573, § 3.

The present writer is inclined however to agree with those who consider the judicial power of the *vice-officialis* to be ordinary power, and accordingly includes that office within the category of offices with reference to whose incumbents the act of removal from office is directly and juridically governed by the provisions of canon 192, § 3.

That these officials can be removed *ad nutum* by the bishop is clearly stated in the Code.[37] But they do not lose their office when the see becomes vacant nor can they be removed from office by the cathedral chapter or by the diocesan consultors, nor by the vicar capitular or the diocesan administrator, except by way of a judicial sentence in a trial for a crime they have committed.[38] Their removal, like that of the vicar general, must be undertaken without the accompaniment of injury to their character or of disgrace for their good name, even though it may be effected *ad nutum.*[39]

Article IV. The Canon Penitentiary

Although the office of canon penitentiary is an unfamiliar position in this country, nevertheless some consideration must be given to this truly ecclesiastical office which is dealt with specifically by the Code in canons 398, 399 and 401. The position itself is one of the major offices distributed among the canons of the cathedral chapter, and is conferred on one who is already a canon. That it fulfills the requirements for an office in the strict sense is clear from the Code itself, especially since the law attaches to this office the *ordinary* power of absolving all, even strangers in the diocese, from sins—even from sins and censures reserved to the bishop.[40]

Can the bishop dislodge the canon penitentiary from his office through an act of simple removal? The Code is silent on this particular point. Since the office as such is conferred on one who is already a canon, it seems that, by the fact that the bishop is the one who confers this office (*audito Capitulo*),[41] he can remove the

[37] Canon 1573, § 5: "Sunt amovibiles ad nutum Episcopi."

[38] Roberti, *De Processibus,* I, n. 99. Cf. also canons 1573, § 5; 2298, 6°.

[39] Coronata, *Institutiones,* III, 27.

[40] Canon 401, § 1.

[41] Canon 403.

incumbent without the need of observing any definite process. For the office of canon penitentiary is, it seems, a position added to the position and office which the incumbent already possesses as a canon of the chapter. As a canon he already is the possessor of a benefice, and thus it seems altogether uncalled for to elevate the office of canon penitentiary into the estate of a benefice distinct from that of the canonry itself. If then the position of canon penitentiary is a simple office, whose incumbent is nowhere in the Code called irremovable, the conclusion follows that the bishop can remove him from the specific position canon penitentiary through an act of simple removal in virtue of the power given in canon 192, § 3.

However, should the office of canon penitentiary at the same time be a benefice, then the manner in which the incumbent may be removed from it will depend on whether that benefice in itself is one whose incumbent is irremovable or removable. If he is irremovable, then the incumbent can be deprived of his office in the strict sense of a privation, that is, as a penalty resulting from a judicial trial, but only for the causes expressly acknowledged in the law, for example, for the non-observance of the law of residence.[42]

If, on the other hand, the benefice is one whose incumbent is removable, then the canon penitentiary could be removed from it for other reasonable causes, and hence it seems that the principle of canon 192, § 3, would apply in such an instance.[43] But, since the bishop confers all benefices and canonries in both cathedral and collegiate churches *audito Capitulo,* it seems implicitly insinuated by the law that the removal likewise should be undertaken *audito Capitulo.*[44] Such a restriction in no way cancels out the permissibility of an act of simple removal; it merely implies that the act of removal is not exercisable *ad nutum.*

Article V. The Vicars Forane

Whether or not the position of vicar forane is an office in the strict sense is a much disputed point among the authors. Some

---

[42] Canon 2299, § 1; Wernz, *Ius Decretalium,* II, tit. XXXVI, n. 796.

[43] Canon 2299, § 1.

[44] Canon 403.

claim that these vicars have ordinary power of jurisdiction.[45] Others equally contend that they have only a delegated power.[46] Still others make a distinction.

Cappello holds that the vicars forane have only administrative or disciplinary power from the common law, but that by particular law whether in consequence of a plenary or a provincial council, or of a diocesan synod, or of some special authoritative intervention on the part of the bishop, they also can have true jurisdiction. The same jurisdiction is ordinary or delegated depending on whether it has been attached to the office itself by the law or committed to the person of the vicar.[47] Chelodi, making somewhat the same distinction, hesitates to call the power which is granted to the vicar forane a true jurisdiction, and maintains that this power reflects rather the prerogative of an official inspecting and reporting than the possession of a true power of jurisdiction.[48] The core of the dispute is the determination on the exact nature of the powers given to vicars forane in canons 447-449. If these powers can be considered as falling within the concept of jurisdiction, then certainly vicars forane have ordinary jurisdiction, and therefore an office in the strict sense.

For the same reasons that were given above concerning the position of the diocesan chancellor,[49] the writer is inclined to agree with those authors who maintain that the vicars forane have an ordinary power of jurisdiction. For they participate to some extent in the administrative non-judicial power of the bishop, a power which is indeed included under the generic term of jurisdiction or *regimen*.[50] Therefore it seems that vicars forane have definite

[45] Maroto, *Institutiones,* I, n. 700; Wernz-Vidal, *Ius Canonicum,* II, n. 716; Zaplotnik, *De Vicariis Foraneis,* pp. 69, 70, 73, 76.

[46] De Meester, *Compendium,* II, 239; Vermeersch-Creusen, *Epitome,* I, n. 532; Beste, *Introductio in Codicem,* p. 215; McBride, *Incardination and Excardination of Seculars,* p. 476.

[47] *Summa Iuris Canonici,* I, 435.

[48] *Ius de Personis,* n. 221.

[49] Cf. *supra,* pp. 90-91.

[50] "Nullam habent potestatem iudicialem, neque legiferam, neque gratiosam. Habent autem semper aliquam potestatem *administrativam,* quoniam possunt et debent aliquando sacerdotes sibi subiectos tractare et paterno modo monere praesertim circa conservationem et administrationem bonorum ecclesiasticorum et similia."—Zaplotnik, *De Vicariis Foraneis,* p. 70.

powers of jurisdiction annexed by the common law to their office. Since this is ordinary power, they are incumbents of an office in the strict sense.

As to their removal from office, the vicars forane can be removed *ad nutum Episcopi,* and therefore through an act of simple removal.[51] Nevertheless, though no cause is necessary for the validity of the removal, natural equity must be observed, and therefore care must be taken lest the stigma of shame or the loss of his good reputation befall the removed vicar when he is removed apart from any fault.[52]

Cappello holds that if the position of vicar forane has by custom been attached to some parish by reason of age or dignity, then the bishop when removing the vicar forane may follow one of three alternatives. He may remove the pastor from the parish, if there are just causes, according to the norms for the administrative removal of pastors, or he may by derogating from the aforesaid custom deprive him solely of the office of the vicar forane, or, finally he may altogether abolish a custom of this kind, and thus the pastor would be deprived of the office of vicar forane.[53]

Causes which would justify the removal of a vicar forane are: want of the knowledge required for the proper fulfillment of his duties, negligence of duties or of the law of residence after one or two warnings,[54] permanent infirmity of body or mind, the good of the vicar forane himself, and, finally, whatever in the prudent judgment of the ordinary yields to the utility of the Church and the benefit of souls.[55]

Article VI. Pastors

There is no problem in identifying the position of pastor as an office in the strict sense. The common law in the Code has per-

---

[51] Canon 446, § 2: "Vicarius foraneus ad nutum Episcopi amoveri potest."

[52] Cappello, *Summa Iuris Canonici,* I, 437; Chelodi, *Ius de Personis,* n. 222, footnote n. 5; Sipos, *Enchiridion,* p. 290; Coronata, *Institutiones,* I, 559; Zaplotnik, *De Vicariis Foraneis,* p. 64.

[53] *Loc. cit.*

[54] Cf. canon 448, § 2.

[55] Zaplotnik, *op. cit.,* p. 64.

petually constituted the position in its generic form,[56] governs the conferring of it,[57] and has attached to it a participation in the power, both of orders and of jurisdiction in the internal forum, which accordingly exists as an ordinary power of jurisdiction.[58]

Not all pastors are subject to a possible loss of their office through the act of a simple removal from it. Most, in fact, can be removed only by means of a trial, that is, through deprivation of office in the strict sense, or, outside of the case of crime, by means of the administrative removal process as regulated by canons 2157-2161 for removable pastors. Even quasi-pastors in a vicariate or a prefecture apostolic are not subject to dislodgment from their office through the act of simple removal.[59] While it is true that the Code states in canon 454, § 4, that these are removable, still that does not mean that they are removable *ad nutum*. The canon just mentioned distinguishes three classes of pastors: those who are irremovable, those who are removable,[60] and those who are removable *ad nutum*.[61] Religious pastors are spoken of as removable *ad nutum*, but quasi-pastors simply as removable. Hence unless the quasi-pastors are also religious, they can be removed only in accordance with the procedure which the law has established for the removal of removable pastors.[62] This is confirmed by the words of canon 192, § 3, which preclude the possibility for removable pastors (the term "removable" being unqualified) to become dispossessed of their office by way of simple removal, since they are made removable only *ad normam iuris*.[63]

Subsequent to the promulgation of the Code some doubt existed for a few years with regard to the status of removable pastors in the United States, since, in virtue of the decree *Maxima cura*, their status remained unchanged. Thus they continued as vicars of their

---

[56] Canon 451.

[57] Canons 453; 455; 459.

[58] Canons 461; 462; 873, § 1; 1044; 1045, § 3; 1245, § 1.

[59] Cf. canons 216, §§ 2, 3; 451, 2, 1°.

[60] Canon 454, §§ 2, 4.

[61] Canon 454, § 5.

[62] Canons 2157-2161; Connor, *The Administrative Removal of Pastors*, p. 14.

[63] Canon 192, § 3: ". . . salvo canonum praescripto circa paroecias amovbiles."

ordinaries, and were removable *ad nutum.*[64] Again, a later reply declared that the decree *Maxima cura* did not give greater permanency to these pastors.[65] However, that their status of permanency was definitely established by the Code of Canon Law is evident from the reply of the Commission for the Authentic Interpretation of the Code to the Apostolic Delegate in the United States.[66] This reply affirmed the fact that all parishes of the United States, if erected with definite boundaries and with a rector assigned to take charge of the people and the church within the said limits, became canonical parishes *ipso facto* on the promulgation of the new Code.

The only pastors, then, who are subject to a possible loss of their office through an act of simple removal without process are those who belong to some religious institute. For such pastors, according to canon 454, § 5, are removable ad nutum.[67] They are always removable *ad nutum,* that is as far as the person of the incumbent is concerned (ratione personae). Both the local ordinary and the competent religious superior enjoy an equal right in this matter, and although neither needs the consent of the other, still each is bound to advise the other superior of his action. This right does not permit any arbitrary use of the power, but implies that it be exercised with equity and charity so that, in so far as is possible, the good name of the pastor is kept intact both with regard to his religious superior, if the local ordinary makes the removal, or vice versa, and with regard to the people.[68]

---

[64] S.C. Consist., decr. *Maxima cura,* 20 aug. 1910—*AAS,* II (1910), 636.

[65] S.C. Consist., 28 iun. 1915—*AAS,* VII (1915), 380.

[66] (Private): Letter of the Apostolic Delegate, Nov. 10, 1922—Bouscaren, *The Canon Law Digest,* I, 149.

[67] "Parochi autem, ad religiosam familiam pertinentes, sunt semper, ratione personae, amovibiles ad nutum tam loci Ordinarii, monito Superiore, quam Superioris, monito Ordinario, aequo iure, non requisito alterius consensu: nec alter alteri causam iudicii sui aperire multoque minus probare tenetur, salvo recursu in devolutivo ad Apostolicam Sedem." The writer is of the opinion that pastors who are members of quasi-religious societies will also come under this norm whenever there is question of their removal from office.

[68] Vermeersch-Creusen, *Epitome,* I, n. 540; Beste, *Introductio in Codicem,* p. 286.

Moreover, the existence of a just and reasonable cause for the removal is supposed by the Code itself. For the canon in question[69] merely states that either superior, that is, the local ordinary or the religious superior, does not have to manifest this cause or reason to the other, much less is either bound to vindicate his reason, save in the event of a non-suspensive recourse, when his reasons must be manifested to the Holy See.[70] Should a clash ensue therefore between the two superiors over such a removal, the last and only remedy is recourse in *devolutivo tantum* to Rome. The local ordinary makes his recourse to the Sacred Congregation of the Council, and the religious superior interposes it with the Sacred Congregation of Religious.[71] The religious pastor who is removed likewise has a right to institute a recourse with the Holy See.[72]

Article VII. The Parochial Vicars of Canon 471.

It may happen that a parish is united in full right (*pleno iure*) to a religious house, to a cathedral or a collegiate chapter, or to some other moral person. In such a case the moral person holds the title to the parish, but a vicar is constituted to exercise the actual parochial care inherent in that title.[73]

From the Code it is apparent that such a parochial vicar has an office in the strict sense. According to canon 471, the position is generically established in a permanent fashion by the common law, its conferral follows the norms of the same law, and it includes from the Code itself a participation in the power of orders and of jurisdiction in the internal forum. For the vicar has the full care of souls, with the rights and obligations of a pastor, according to the approved diocesan statutes or laudable customs.[74] Hence his power of jurisdiction is ordinary.[75]

---

[69] Canon 454, § 5.

[70] Vermeersch-Creusen, *Epitome,* I, 540; Coronata, *Institutiones,* I, 569, footnote n. 5.

[71] Augustine, *A Commentary on Canon Law,* II, 521.

[72] Beste, *op. cit.,* p. 286.

[73] Canons 452, § 2; 471, § 1.

[74] Canon 471, § 4.

[75] De Meester, *Compendium,* II, 332.

The details of the removal of such a parochial vicar are respectively different, according to whether it is a religious house to which the parish is united, or some other moral person. If the vicar is a religious, then he is removable in the same manner as the religious pastor, that is *ad nutum* of either the local ordinary or the religious superior, as long as a just cause is present and equity is duly observed.[76]

But if the vicar is in charge of a parish which is united to another moral person, then once he is appointed he is not removable at all by the moral person, and can be removed by the ordinary only through the process of law as required for the removal of other pastors, but not through an act of simple removal.[77] Whether he is irremovable or removable depends upon the degree of stability in his office as deriving from the status of the parish whose actual care is committed to him.[78] However, the ordinary is bound to notify the person who presented the vicar concerning the removal.[79]

Article VIII. Other Parochial Vicars

In addition to the office of parochial vicar of moral persons, there are other vicars specified in the Code under the name of parochial vicars. These are: the vicar econome (or more commonly in this country called the administrator) of a vacant parish;[80] the vicar substitute, who is designated to take the place of a pastor who will be absent from his parish beyond a week, or of a pastor who has been deprived of his office by judicial decree and has appealed to the Holy See;[81] the vicar adjutant (or coadjutor), who supplies for a pastor who is permanently incapacitated for some cause such as old age, blindness, etc.;[82] and finally the vicar assistant, who is assigned to help a pastor who, because of the multitude of the people or for other causes, cannot handle a parish alone.[83] The position of each of these vicars shall be considered

[76] Canon 471, § 3; 454, § 5.

[77] Canon 471, § 3.

[78] Connor, *The Administrative Removal of Pastors,* p. 10.

[79] Canon 471, § 3.

[80] Canon 472.

[81] Canon 474.

[82] Canon 475, § 1.

[83] Canon 476, § 1.

first, and then their removal from office, since the same regulations apply to all of them.

1—The vicar econome or administrator of a vacant parish.—Although some authors, such as Blat,[84] maintain that the power of jurisdiction of the vicar econome is delegated by the law (*ad universitatem negotiorum*), since it is not attached to an office which in a strict sense is permanently constituted, most authors concede that this office implies ordinary power, inasmuch as the power of this office is by law itself attached to the latter, which the law has created with a status of objective stability, and the conferral of which the law calls for under plainly specified circumstances.[85] This teaching, it seems, is confirmed by the Code when a comparison is made between canon 451, § 2, 2°, where it is stated that parochial vicars who are endowed with full parochial power are equal to pastors and in law are included under the name of pastor,[86] and canon 873, § 1, where it is stated that those who are in the place of pastors enjoy ordinary jurisdiction for the hearing of confessions in their territory.[87]

2—The vicar substitute.—The same remarks can be made about the vicar who is appointed according to the norms of canon 465, §§ 4, 5[88] and canon 1923, § 2,[89] for the Code states clearly that he takes the place of the pastor in everything which relates to the care

[84] *Commentarium,* II, 440.

[85] De Meester, *Compendium,* II, 333; Cappello, *Summa Iuris Canonici,* I, 509; Beste, *Introductio in Codicem,* p. 214; Bouscaren-Ellis, *Canon Law,* p. 220.

[86] "Parochis aequiparantur et . . . parochorum nomine in iure veniunt: . . . Vicarii paroeciales, si plena potestate paroeciali sint praediti."

[87] "Ordinaria iurisdictione ad confessiones excipiendas . . . potiuntur . . . pro suo quisque territorio . . . aliique qui loco parochi sunt."

[88] "Sive continuum sive intermissum sit vacationis tempus, cum absentia ultra hebdomadam est duratura, parochus, praeter legitimam causam, habere debet Ordinarii scriptam licentiam et vicarium substitutum sui loco relinquere ab eodem Ordinario probandum; . . .

"Si parochus repentina et gravi causa discedere atque ultra hebdomadam cogatur abesse, quamprimum per litteras Ordinarium commonefaciat, ei indicans causam discessus et sacerdotem supplentem, eiusque stet mandatis."

[89] "Ad exsecutionem privationis beneficii iudex ne procedat contra clericum qui Sanctam Sedem adierit; sed si agatur de beneficio, cui adnexa sit animarum cura, Ordinarius provideat per designationem vicarii substituti."

of souls unless the local ordinary or the pastor have made some exceptions.[90] Hence, in the absence of any special restrictions by either, he has the full and ordinary jurisdiction of a pastor, provided he is taking his place for more than a week.[91]

3—The vicar adjutant.—This parochial vicar is appointed as a coadjutor to a pastor who, by reason of old age, weakness of mind, want of learning, blindness or some other permanent cause, becomes unable to perform his duties. Whether he is appointed to supply for the incapacitated pastor in whole or in part will determine whether or not he has an office in the strict sense. The Code provides for both types of position.[92]

If the parochial adjutant supplies for the pastor in all things, then he has from the Code itself all the power of a pastor,[93] and hence ordinary power of jurisdiction in the internal forum—hence an office in the strict sense.[94] But if he is to supply for the pastor only in part, his powers are delegated through his letter of appointment.[95] Consequently, in view of the stand taken by the present writer, his position is not an office in the strict sense.

4—The vicar assistant.—The position of vicar assistant, or, as he is more commonly called, the assistant pastor, can hardly be regarded as an office in the strict sense, that is, in view of what was maintained in a preceding chapter concerning the participation in the power of Orders or of jurisdiction as a requisite for an office in the strict sense.[96] For, as far as the power of Orders is concerned, the assistant's sphere of activity does not seem inherently to call for the exercise of the power of Orders in any specific manner, so that the content of his office would involve his participation in the power of Orders. As to jurisdiction, it is clear that whatever power the assistant enjoys is delegated. The Code states that his

[90] Canon 474: "Vicarius substitutus . . . locum parochi tenet in omnibus quae ad curam animarum spectant, nisi. . . ." Cf. De Meester, *op. cit.*, II, 335; Cappello, *op. cit.*, I, 510; Beste, *loc. cit.*

[91] Bouscaren-Ellis, *op. cit.*, p. 221.

[92] Canon 475, §§ 1, 2.

[93] Canon 475, § 2.

[94] Cf. canons 451, § 2; 873, § 1; De Meester, *op. cit.*, II, 337; Chelodi, *Ius de Personis*, n. 230; Cappello, *op. cit.*, I, 510; Bouscaren-Ellis, *op. cit.*, p. 223.

[95] Canon 475, § 2; De Meester, *loc. cit.*; Chelodi, *loc. cit.*

[96] Cf. *supra*, pp. 56-58; 58-60.

rights and powers are to be determined and delegated by the diocesan statutes, by the letters of the ordinary, and by the pastor.[97]

It is of the very nature of the position of the assistant pastor, not to imply a complete supplanting of the pastor in his work, but rather to connote the lending of help to a pastor who is present and actually performing his share of the parochial duties. Though the assistant does not have an office in the strict sense, the writer has included the consideration of his position at this particular point in the present work, because of the logical sequence the Code gives to all parochial vicars, and especially since the Code enacts the same regulation for all these offices with regard to the removal of their incumbents from them.

Removal.—The parochial vicars mentioned in canons 472-476 are all removable through an act of simple removal. If they are members of a religious community, they can be removed *ad nutum* by the local ordinary or the competent religious superior in the same manner as religious pastors, according to canon 454, § 5.[98] But if the vicars are seculars, they are removable *ad nutum* by the bishop or the vicar capitular (or the diocesan administrator), but not by the vicar general unless he have a special mandate.[99]

Just as in the removal of the vicar general, so too in the removal of these parochial vicars, a reasonable, though not grave, cause is required for the lawfulness of the act of removal.[100] Ayrinhac (1867-1930) included among the reasonable motives for removal the promotion of the vicar, the good of a particular parish, or the general good of the diocese, and noted that the Church does not approve of arbitrary or unreasonably frequent changes.[101] Never-

---

[97] Canon 476, § 6; compare with canons 451, § 2, and 873, § 1. Cf. also Cappello, *op. cit.*, I, 512; De Meester, *op. cit.*, II, 340, especially where the author notes: ". . . ministerium eius non est officium strictum," *ibid.*, p. 342; Chelodi, *op. cit.*, n. 232; Bouscaren-Ellis, *op. cit.*, p. 224; Bastnagel, *The Appointment of Parochial Adjutants and Assistants*, pp. 141-144. For a lengthy explanation of the contrary opinion, the reader is referred to McBride, *Incardination and Excardination of Seculars*, pp. 486-488.

[98] Canon 477, § 1.

[99] Canon 477, § 1.

[100] Cappello, *Summa Iuris Canonici*, I, 514.

[101] *Constitution of the Church in the New Code of Canon Law* (New York: Benziger & Co., 1925), p. 365.

theless the removal cannot generally be said to be invalid if it is done without any just cause, even if done out of fraud and hatred, and even with grave harm to the incumbent who is removed.[102]

One exception is made by the Code itself in canon 477, § 2, to the simple removal of a parochial vicar. That exception is the parochial assistant whose assistant pastorate is a benefice. It is important to indicate briefly in what sense this can be possible.[103]

The office of assistant pastor in the sense of canon 476 is not and cannot be meant here. For that office in its specific form neither has nor can have objective perpetuity, for the simple reason that a limit is set to its existence by the law itself. It is by its very nature temporary to take care of certain needs. Even though the need may be foreseen to be of indefinite duration, the essential nature of the office is not thereby changed. Since then an assistant pastorate in the sense of canon 476 has no objective perpetuity, it cannot be erected into a benefice.[104] Canon 1412, 1°, shows that a parochial vicarage can be a benefice only when it is erected in perpetuity in a particular place.[105]

Since an assistancy or vicarage in the sense of canon 476 cannot meet the requirements, in what sense is it posssible? Canon 1427 gives the answer. When the ordinary, for reasons given in the same canon, divides a parish, and consequently a parochial benefice, two benefices result,[106] the newer of which may take one of two forms. If the proper conditions are present, he may erect a new parish, presided over by a real pastor, and then it is an independent entity. If, however, the conditions do not warrant the erection of a new parish, then the ordinary may simply erect a perpetual vicarage, that is, he may designate a second church and perpetually establish there the office of a vicar, with the care of

---

[102] Wernz-Vidal, *Ius Canonicum,* II, n. 744; Coronata, *Institutiones,* I, 598, footnote n. 3.

[103] For a lengthy treatment on this question, which would be beyond the purpose of this work, the reader is referred to McBride, *Incardination and Excardination of Seculars,* pp. 488-503.

[104] Canon 1409; McBride, *op. cit.,* p. 488.

[105] "Licet aliquam cum beneficiis similitudinem praeseferant, in iure tamen beneficii nomine non veniunt:

1°. Vicariae paroeciales non in perpetuum erectae";

[106] Canon 1421.

souls, and the consequent obligation of residence. This new benefice is united by subjection to the mother church (*unione minus principali*),[107] so that the pastor of the parish becomes the pastor of the filial church,[108] and the resident vicar who is perpetually constituted there becomes subject to him.[109] Such a vicarage is in reality therefore an assistant pastorate. The vicar is really linked with the parish, and has no proper power from the Code, but is the vicar of, and subject to, the pastor. He is a *vicarius cooperator* endowed with the added qualifications which the application of canon 1427 implies in the case, that is, his office is objectively perpetual, and a benefice.

Consequently the perpetual assistant vicar cannot be removed by means of an act of simple removal, but only according to the norms of law and for the causes for which other pastors whether removable or irremovable can be removed, with the added cause of grave insubordination to the pastor in the exercise of his functions —for which cause, it may be noted, he can be removed by an administrative process.[110] However, it seems that if the ordinary had obtained a special indult in virtue of which such benefices could be conferred as revocable *ad nutum,* then the ordinary could remove the vicar *ad nutum,* provided there is a reasonable cause and equity is observed.[111]

Article IX. Chaplains

Definite positions of chaplains, that is, of priests who, in virtue of the position which they obtain, have the right and duty to perform certain spiritual functions for the benefit of particular individuals or groups of persons, are established either directly or

---

[107] Canon 1419, 3°.

[108] Canon 1420, § 3.

[109] Cf. Pistocchi, *De Re Beneficiali iuxta Canones Codicis Iuris Canonici* (Taurini: Marietti, 1928), pp. 114-116 (hereafter cited *De Re Beneficiali*).

[110] Canon 477, § 2: "Quod si vicaria sit beneficialis, vicarius cooperator removeri potest processu ad normam iuris, non solum ob causas propter quas alii parochi removeri possunt, sed etiam si graviter subiectioni parocho debitae in exercitio suarum functionum." Cf. Connor, *The Administrative Removal of Pastors,* p. 80.

[111] Canon 1438.

implicitly by the Code of Canon Law.[112] There are chaplains of lay religious institutes; chaplains of pious associations of the faithful, particularly of confraternities and pious unions; chaplains of non-collegiate ecclesiastical institutes, such as hospitals; and simple Mass chaplains.[113]

Concerning the office of chaplain of non-exempt lay religious institutes, whether of men or of women, it is important, in order to determine whether the office is one in the strict sense, to establish that the bishop has removed these houses from the care of the pastor in whose territory the houses are situated, and appointed over them a chaplain subject directly to himself. The power to do just that is given the bishop in canon 464, § 2, and the chaplain who is thus appointed obtains from the Code itself the right to administer Holy Viaticum and Extreme Unction to the sick and dying.[114] Consequently he may be said to have an office in the strict sense.

As to the removal of these chaplains, a distinction must be made. The Code contains no specific regulation about their removal. However, the law does state that it is the local ordinary who designates the chaplain for a non-exempt lay religious institute.[115] Hence it seems that it pertains to the same ordinary to effect the removal, which can be done by means of an act of simple removal in virtue of canon 192, § 3. With regard to the chaplain of an exempt lay religious community however, that is a chaplain who does not enjoy parochial power, it is the regular religious superior who designates the chaplain. Accordingly it seems logical to conclude that, in view of the exemption which the institute enjoys, it is within the power of the proper religious superior according to the norms of the constitutions to decree the removal of the chaplain, rather than within the power of the local ordinary, at least as far as the act of a simple removal from the office is concerned.[116]

With regard to the chaplains of pious associations of the faithful,

---

[112] Canon 479, § 2; De Meester, *Compendium,* II, 359.

[113] Another group of chaplains known as military chaplains are regulated as to their rights and duties by special prescripts of the Holy See.—Canon 451, § 3.

[114] Canon 514, § 3.

[115] Canon 529.

[116] Cf. canon 529.

that is, strictly ecclesiastical associations, canon 700 states that there are three species: third Orders secular, confraternities, and pious unions. Unless there is an apostolic privilege to the contrary, the nomination of the chaplain for those associations which have been erected or approved by the local ordinary or by the Apostolic See, and also for the associations erected by religious in virtue of an apostolic privilege outside their own churches, rests with the local ordinary; in associations, however, erected by the religious in their own churches, the consent of the local ordinary is required only if the religious superior appoints a chaplain from among the secular clergy.[117]

The office itself is a true ecclesiastical office in the strict sense, for it is constituted by the common law, is conferred according to the norms of the same law, has stability, and participates in the exercise of the power of Orders. The chaplain receives from the law itself the faculty of blessing the habit, the insignia, the scapulars, etc., of the association—hence an ordinary power.[118]

There is no doubt that the local ordinary can by means of an act of simple removal remove for a just cause those chaplains who were appointed by himself. Religious superiors likewise can remove those chaplains whom they designated for the office.[119] It seems from the law itself that the local ordinary cannot through an act of simple removal remove the chaplain who was appointed by the religious superiors from among their own clergy. With regard however to a chaplain who is selected from among the secular clergy, it seems logical, in view of the local ordinary's jurisdiction over his own clergy, and in view of canon 192, § 3, that he can remove this chaplain, but he should then notify the proper religious superior of his action. Likewise, if the religious superior wishes to remove this chaplain whom he indeed appointed, but only upon the previous consent of the bishop, it seems logical that

[117] Canon 698, § 1.

[118] Canon 698, § 2; Cappello, *Summa Iuris Canonici,* II (ed. 4., Romae, 1945), 113; Clarke, *Parish Societies,* The Catholic University of America Canon Law Studies, n. 176 (Washington, D. C.: The Catholic University of America Press, 1943), p. 85.

[119] Canon 698, § 3: "Moderatorem et cappellanum revocare ex iusta causa possunt qui illos nominaverunt eorumque successores vel Superiores."

he should notify the bishop of the fact. The Code itself is silent on this question, but, in the mind of the writer, an analogy may be drawn from the norms of the Code regarding the removal of religious pastors.[120]

The third group of chaplains presents the problem whether their appointment connotes the holding of an office in the strict sense. Some authors, such as McBride, include these chaplains, e.g., hospital chaplains, chaplains of orphanages, of schools, etc., under the same category as the chaplains appointed in the houses of non-exempt lay religious, provided the ordinary has in virtue of canon 464, § 2, exempted the respective institutes from the care of the local pastor in the same way as he can do for the non-exempt lay religious institutes.[121] Once the ordinary has exempted the hospital, orphanage or school from the care of the local pastor, and appointed a chaplain over the institute, McBride infers that the chaplain thereby obtains from the Code itself the powers granted in canon 514, § 3.[122]

But the opinion that these chaplains do not have an office in the strict sense, as explained by Drumm in his work *Hospital Chaplains,* seems the more forceful.[123] The author argues that canon 464, § 2, implies the establishment of the position of a chaplain, and indeed canon 514, § 3, which is concerned with the chaplains of lay religious communities, names that chaplain explicitly. Yet the position of chaplains such as hospital chaplains, as distinct from that of the chaplain of a lay religious community, is nowhere mentioned in the Code, but only implied in the right of the bishop to withdraw pious houses, including hospitals, from the pastor's jurisdiction.[124] It is not correct, Drumm maintains, to say that such a chaplain merely by reason of the exemption of the institution can perform pastoral functions. Rather, it is the faculty which the

---

[120] Canon 454, § 5; cf. *supra,* pp. 65-67.

[121] McBride, *Incardination and Excardination of Seculars,* p. 506.

[122] It must be remembered also that McBride holds the opinion which considers delegated power sufficient for an office in the strict sense—*Op. cit.,* p. 446.

[123] The Catholic University of America Canon Law Studies, n. 178 (Washington, D. C.: The Catholic University of America Press, 1943), pp. 61-64.

[124] *Op. cit.,* p. 60.

bishop has under canon 464, § 2, which implies the right to depute or delegate a priest as chaplain to perform these exempt functions.[125] Hence the chaplain administers to his subjects by reason of delegation received either from the bishop or from particular law. But such a chaplain, as distinct from the chaplain of religious communities, has no powers whatsoever from the common law.

The present writer favors this latter opinion. Hence, as far as the simple removal of these chaplains by the ordinary is concerned, the conclusion must be that these offices do not come directly or juridically under the provisions of canon 192, § 3. Nevertheless, by analogy it can be argued that the removal from these positions is to be regulated by the same principles and, therefore, that a just cause must be present and equity must be observed.

Chaplains of the fourth group are known as simple Mass chaplains. In virtue of their office they have the right to celebrate Mass in the church or chapel where they are located. As was pointed out in a preceding chapter, they participate to a sufficient extent in the power of Orders that they can be considered as the occupants of ecclesiastical offices in the strict sense.[126] Examples of such chaplains are the priests appointed as chaplains of domestic or private oratories.[127] There seems no doubt that the ordinary can remove these chaplains according to the norms of canon 192, § 3.

However, it is possible for such a chaplaincy to be erected also into a benefice. The chaplaincy in this sense may be defined as a pious assignment, to be conferred on some cleric, consisting of the obligation of celebrating Mass on stated days at some altar or in some church, and of performing such other sacred duties as may be enjoined, together with the right of receiving the revenues from an endowment given by the founder.[128] Provided that the endowment has passed into the possession of the church, and that the creation of the assignment has been effected by means of a formal decree issued on the bishop's authority, the chaplaincy is an ecclesiastical chaplaincy and a benefice.

---

[125] *Op. cit.*, p. 64.

[126] Cf. *supra*, pp. 56-58.

[127] Cf. canon 1195.

[128] Pistocchi, *De Re Beneficiali*, p. 33.

The removal of the incumbent will then depend on whether the benefice is perpetual or revocable at will. Objectively of course it is erected in perpetuity, but subjectively, that is, as far as the incumbent is concerned, the chaplaincy may be either perpetual or manual, since subjective perpetuity in office does not pertain to the essential nature of a benefice.[129] If the chaplaincy is perpetual so that its incumbent is irremovable, then the incumbent can be removed only by means of an act of strict privation and for the reasons expressed in the law; but if it is manual so that its incumbent is removable, then he can be deprived of his office by the ordinary for other reasonable causes in the form of a vindictive penalty for some crime.[130] Likewise, aside from any crime or fault on the part of the incumbent, the ordinary can remove the chaplain by means of an act of simple removal according to the provisions of canon 192, § 3, provided that the benefice has been conferred as a manual, or revocable at will, benefice.

Article X. Seminary Rectors

The Code of Canon Law establishes permanently the position of rector of a seminary,[131] and gives the norms to be followed in its conferral.[132] Moreover, from the common law itself it is clear that the rector has an office in the strict sense, for the seminary is exempt from the jurisdiction of the pastor in whose territory it is situated, and the rector fulfills the office of pastor over all those who dwell within the seminary, with the exception of certain restrictions concerning the sacraments of matrimony and of penance.[133] The rector has the right therefore to administer the sacraments, including Viaticum and extreme unction;[134] to dispense from the laws of fast and abstinence, and from the observance of

[129] Canon 1411, 4°.

[130] Canon 2299, § 1.

[131] Canon 1358.

[132] Canon 1360, § 1.

[133] Canon 1368: "Exemptum a iurisdictione paroeciali Seminarium esto; et pro omnibus qui in Seminario sunt, parochi officium, excepta materia matrimoniali et firmo praescripto can. 891, obeat Seminarii rector eiusve delegatus, nisi in quibusdam Seminariis fuerit aliter a Sede Apostolica constitutum."

[134] Cf. canons 850; 958, § 2.

feasts of obligation,[135] and to perform the usual funeral services under the accompaniment of all the rights and duties attached thereto.[136]

Cappello notes that the rector is freely nominated by the bishop after consultation with the deputies or board of discipline which the Code in canon 1359 requires to be established.[137] The same author,[138] and also Cox, in his work *The Administration of Seminaries,*[139] maintains that the bishop has the right to remove the rector and other seminary officials whenever he so desires, hence by means of an act of simple removal, provided that such a removal is effected for a just cause, and equity is observed. Cox also lists some just causes for the removal. These causes are: chronic illness, old age, discord among the officials themselves, or between the rector and the students, bad example on the part of the rector, the necessity of transferring the rector to another position, the promotion of the incumbent, the refusal by the incumbent, after an admonition, to make the usual profession of faith as required by canon 2403, and finally heterodoxy, or even the suspicion of it, especially with reference to Modernism.[140] But the rector may against the decree of the bishop institute a recourse to the Sacred Congregation of Seminaries and Universities.[141]

Article XI. Rectors of Churches

The term "rector" of a church signifies in law a priest who has charge of a church which is neither parochial, nor capitular, nor annexed to the house of a religious community for the purpose of celebrating therein the divine offices.[142] The position itself seems to be an office in the strict sense: it is permanently established by

---

[135] Canon 1245, § 1.

[136] Canon 1222.

[137] *Summa Iuris Canonici,* II, 495; cf. canon 1359, § 4, which demands that the bishop seek the advice of the deputies in matters of weighty importance.

[138] *Loc. cit.*

[139] The Catholic University of America Canon Law Studies, n. 67 (Washington, D. C.: The Catholic University of America, 1931), p. 80.

[140] *Op. cit.,* pp. 80, 93.

[141] *Op. cit.,* p. 80.

[142] Canon 479, § 1.

the Code, it is conferred according to the norms of the same law,[143] and, although it does not participate in the power of jurisdiction,[144] it does carry with it some participation in the power of Orders, namely, in the right to celebrate in the church the divine offices,[145] with the exception of those functions which are reserved to the pastor.[146]

The local ordinary may *ad nutum* remove the rector for any just cause, even though he has been elected or presented by others. Those, however, who presented or elected him cannot remove him.[147] If the rector is a member of a religious community, then both the local ordinary and the competent religious superior enjoy an equal right in this matter, just as they do according to the norms of canon 454, § 5, when there is question of the removal of pastors who belong to a religious community.[148]

SECTION II. INCUMBENTS SUBJECT TO THE PROVISIONS OF CANON 192, § 3, BY ANALOGY

In the preceding section were considered those offices which, being ecclesiastical offices in the strict sense, are juridically subject to the norms of canon 192, § 3, as far as the removal of their incumbents is concerned. It remains to treat of the other offices, that is, of ecclesiastical offices in the wide sense, and of the norms to be followed when there is question of removing the incumbents of these offices. Although these offices do not come directly or juridically under the provisions of simple removal as regulated by canon 192, § 3, nevertheless the present writer maintains that the principles enunciated in that canon are to be applied, in virtue

[143] Canon 480.

[144] De Meester, *Compendium,* II, 357; Cappello, *Summa Iuris Canonici,* I, 516.

[145] Canon 482; McBride, *Incardination and Excardination of Seculars,* p. 504.

[146] Canon 481.

[147] Canon 195.

[148] Canon 486: "Rectorem ecclesiae, etsi ab aliis electum aut praesentatum, Ordinarius loci removere ad nutum potest ex qualibet iusta causa; quod si rector fuerit religiosus, servetur, circa eius remotionem, praescriptum can. 454, § 5.

of canon 20, in the matter of removal from these offices. The latter canon provides that, aside from the matter of canonical penalties, if there is no explicit provision concerning some affairs either in the general or in the particular law, a norm of action is to be taken from laws given in similar cases, from the general principles of law applied with the equity proper to canon law, from the manner and practice of the Roman Curia, and from the common and constant teaching of the doctors.[149]

Whereas canon 192, § 3, allows removal for any cause which the ordinary prudently judges to be a just one, the Code sometimes restricts this broad power in that it requires for the removal from certain offices a grave cause, the consent or advice of others, etc., before the ordinary may decree the removal. Such restrictions do not imply a contradiction in the Code; rather, they indicate that the ordinary, when using the power given him in canon 192, § 3, is to measure the reasonableness or justice of the cause for removal in these particular instances on the basis of what the law itself demands.

Article I. The Notaries

The position of notary in the diocesan curia, whose main duty, as outlined in canon 374, is to draw up various forms of documents, decrees, sentences, and the like, cannot be considered an office in the strict sense. For these duties include neither the power of Orders nor that of jurisdiction.[150] Even Coronata, who, as was already mentioned, implies that the chancellor has some participation in the power of jurisdiction, denies the same with regard to other notaries. For he holds that the office of notary cannot be called a truly ecclesiastical office, that is, in the strict sense.[151]

[149] "Si certa de re desit expressum praescriptum legis sive generalis sive particularis, norma sumenda est, nisi agatur de poenis applicandis, a legibus latis in similibus; a generalibus iuris principiis cum aequitate canonica servatis; a stylo et praxi Curiae Romanae; a communi constantique sententia doctorum."

[150] Roberti, *De Processibus,* I, n. 117; Chelodi, *Ius de Personis,* n. 201.

[151] *Institutiones,* I, 504; cf. also, *op. cit.,* III, 35: "Munus notarii est munus testis qualificati quod nullam proprie dictae iurisdictionis potestatem importat."

Furthermore, the fact that the law permits laymen to hold the office of notary, except in the hearing of criminal cases of clerics, is evident proof that the notary does not enjoy any power of jurisdiction.[152]

Notaries can be removed from office by means of an act of simple removal in the same manner as the chancellor, that is, by the one who appointed them, namely the bishop, or by his successor, or by a higher superior. However they cannot be removed by the vicar capitular or the administrator of a vacant see, except with the consent of the chapter or board of consultors.[153]

In addition to the general duties of a public notary in the diocesan curia, notaries are employed for definite duties in ecclesiastical trials. Thus the Code requires that at every trial there must be present a notary who acts as secretary or clerk, and that the judge before beginning a trial must appoint this secretary from among the notaries legitimately appointed for the diocesan curia, unless the ordinary himself has already designated one for that particular trial.[154]

The question then may be asked: can the judge by means of an act of simple removal remove this notary from his office? It seems that in virtue of the ruling contained in canon 1583 he can remove him in the same way as he is empowered to remove an auditor. That is to say, for a just reason he can remove the notary whom he has appointed for this particular case which he is trying. In other words, the judge cannot remove the notary from his permanent official status as a notary of the curia, but he can remove him from acting as secretary or clerk in the trial in question. This conclusion, it seems, is confirmed by canon 1640, § 2, which states that all persons assisting at a trial who gravely offend against the respect and obedience due to the court, may be at once forced to obey through censures and other appropriate penalties imposed by the judge. Furthermore canon 2220, § 1, empowers those who

---

[152] Canon 118: "Soli clerici possunt potestatem sive ordinis sive iurisdictionis ecclesiasticae . . . obtinere."

[153] Canon 373, § 5: "Omnes possunt removeri aut suspendi ab eo qui illos constituit aut ab eius successore aut Superiore, non autem a Vicario Capitulari, nisi de consensu Capituli"; cf. also canons 105; 373, § 1.

[154] Canon 1585, §§ 1, 2.

possess judicial power to impose by the process of law the penalties legitimately enacted in a law or established by a precept. Hence, if there is question of a grave delict, it seems that the *officialis*—but not however a delegated judge—could even deprive the notary of his very office or status of diocesan notary, not however by means of a simple removal, but in a judicial manner in the strict sense of privation, for example, if the notary had destroyed or substantially altered any document pertaining to the episcopal curia,[155] or if he had presumptuously falsified acts or documents.[156]

Article II. The Synodal Examiners and the Parish Priest Consultors

Canons 385-386 give the norms for the conferral of the offices of synodal examiner and parish priest consultor. However an examination of the duties incumbent upon these officials, as expressed in the law, shows that at no time do they exercise ecclesiastical power, whether of Orders or of jurisdiction. They merely aid in the various clerical examinations, and act as an advisory board to the bishop in various administrative processes.[157]

Concerning their removal from office, the Code very clearly states that they cannot be removed by the bishop except for a grave cause and after he has taken counsel with the cathedral chapter or the diocesan consultors.[158] Connolly notes that in the law prior to the Code the consent of the chapter was required, whereas now obviously only the advice, which the bishop is free either to follow or to forsake, is necessary.[159]

Does the word *"nequeunt"* in canon 388 indicate that both a grave cause and the advice of the chapter or of the diocesan con-

[155] Canon 2045.

[156] Canon 2406.

[157] Cf. canons 389; 2147-2185; Connolly, *Synodal Examiners and Parish Priest Consultors,* The Catholic University of America Canon Law Studies, n. 177 (Washington, D. C.: The Catholic University of America Press, 1943), p. 75.

[158] Canon 388: "Removeri ab Episcopo nequeunt, nisi ex gravi causa et de consilio Capituli cathedralis."

[159] *Op. cit.,* p. 96; cf. canon 105.

sultors are required for validity? Canon 11 states that those laws only are to be considered invalidating which explicitly or equivalently state that an action is null and void.[160] That the word *"nequeunt"* is just such an equivalent of an express statement that an act contrary to this prescription would be invalid is the teaching of Coronata[161] and Cappello.[162] Other authors, however, hold that these conditions are not required for validity, but rather for liceitness.[163]

Just what would constitute a grave cause for a removal is ultimately left to the prudent judgment of the ordinary. Prudence of course dictates that he give serious consideration to the advice of the diocesan consultors in this matter. The cause might be a grave delict on the part of the incumbent, e.g., fraud committed at an examination, or acceptance of a bribe in the removal processes of a pastor,[164] or even something involuntary and blameless, e.g., a lengthy illness.[165] Finally, as Augustine (1872-1943) noted, the reasons which would justify the removal of a pastor would also justify the removal of a synodal examiner or of a parish priest consultor.[166]

Article III. The Synodal and Pro-Synodal Judges

The Code in canon 1574 provides that either in the synod or outside the synod the bishop appoint priests who in consequence of power delegated to them by the bishop are to have a part in judg-

---

[160] "Irritantes . . . eae tantum leges habendae sunt, quibus . . . actum esse nullum . . . expresse vel aequivalenter statuitur."

[161] *Institutiones,* I, 512.

[162] *Summa Iuris Canonici,* I, 367.

[163] Sipos, *Enchiridion Iuris Canonici,* p. 280; Augustine, *A Commentary on Canon Law,* II, 423. The latter author maintained that a removal effected without a solid reason would be valid, provided that the advice of the chapter or the board of consultors had been obtained. Hence he seemed not to require a grave reason for the validity of the removal, but he apparently did always require the advice of the consultors.

[164] Augustine, *loc. cit.;* Connolly, *op. cit.,* p. 97; cf. parallel laws in canons 1625 and 1666 concerning the violation of secrecy and the acceptance of bribes.

[165] Connolly, *loc. cit.*

[166] *Loc. cit.;* cf. canon 2147.

ing disputes. Roberti[167] and McBride[168] maintain that these judges have ordinary power. They base their opinion on the fact that the common law itself attaches to the generic position of synodal and pro-synodal judge the right to give a definitive sentence when acting in a collegiate tribunal. Wernz-Vidal,[169] Cappello,[170] and Dugan,[171] on the other hand, hold that the power these judges obtain is only a delegated power—delegated for a particular time, place and cause. Thus they interpret the words *"potestate ab Episcopo delegata,"* as contained in canon 1574, § 1, to mean that, in virtue of the jurisdiction which they receive from the bishop, the auxiliary judges may assist in the settlement of disputes in ecclesiastical courts.[172] The present writer is inclined to favor this latter opinion. Consequently he regards the office of synodal or pro-synodal judge as an office only in the wide sense.

With regard to their removal, the Code regulates that the judges can be removed in the same way as synodal examiners and parish priest consultors, according to the norms of canon 388.[173] The bishop, then, can for a grave reason remove any one of these judges from office. Before such action, however, he must present the matter for the counsel of the cathedral chapter or of the diocesan consultors.[174]

Article IV. The Auditors

An auditor may be defined as a priest who, by reason of the jurisdiction delegated to him, is empowered to cite witnesses before an ecclesiastical court, hear their testimony, and perform other judicial acts, in keeping with and in the measure of the limits of the commission through which he acts.[175] His power depends almost entirely on the will of the judge.[176]

---

[167] *De Processibus,* I, n. 103.

[168] *Incardination and Excardination of Seculars,* p. 467.

[169] *Ius Canonicum,* VI, n. 90.

[170] *Summa Iuris Canonici,* III, 28.

[171] *The Judiciary Department of the Diocesan Curia,* pp. 42, 44.

[172] Cf. Dugan, *op. cit.,* p. 44.

[173] Canon 1574, § 2: "Quod ad eorum electionem, substitutionem, cessationem aut remotionem a munere attinet, serventur praescripts can. 385-388."

[174] Cf. *supra,* pp. 133-135.

[175] Canons 1581; 1582; Dugan, *op. cit.,* p. 50.

[176] Roberti, *De Processibus,* I, n. 113.

Although the Code, in canon 1582, mentions certain powers which the auditor may exercise, it is disputed among the authors whether this power is ordinary or delegated. Roberti admits that the auditor's powers depend on the will of the judge, but maintains that it does not follow from this fact that the office does not imply the possession of ordinary power. He holds that the auditor possesses ordinary power if he is permanently constituted in the tribunal, but delegated power if he is appointed for individual cases only.[177]

Cappello, making a different distinction, holds that the power annexed to the office itself in virtue of canon 1582 is ordinary, but that other powers which perchance are given to the auditor are delegated.[178] Others, however, such as Wernz-Vidal,[179] Coronata,[180] Beste[181] and Dugan,[182] maintain that the auditor always acts *secundum tenorem mandati,* and hence his power is delegated to him, whether by the ordinary permanently, or by the judge for the particular case which he is trying. Holding to this latter opinion, the present writer concludes that the office of auditor is not an office in the strict sense and accordingly is subject to the provisions of canon 192, § 3, only by analogy.

The auditor can be removed from his office by means of a simple removal at any moment of the process, either before or after the *contestatio litis.* If he has been appointed by the ordinary[183] either permanently or for a definite cause, it is the bishop who removes him. But if the judge has appointed him for a particular trial, then that judge is competent to remove the auditor from office. However, the Code adds that there must be a just cause for the

---

177 *Loc. cit.;* cf. McBride, *Incardination and Excardination of Seculars,* p. 469.

178 *Summa Iuris Canonici,* III, 33.

179 *Ius Canonicum,* VI, n. 100.

180 *Institutiones,* III, 33.

181 *Introductio in Codicem,* p. 769.

182 *Op. cit.,* p. 50; cf. also *ibid.,* p. 53, where the author states that the duties of the auditor must be clearly indicated in the mandate or the appointment, and that the duties mentioned in canon 1582 are those which are usually committed to him.

183 The term "*Ordinarius*" in this matter does not include the vicar general. Cf. Beste, *op. cit.,* pp. 765, 768.

removal, and any prejudice or injury to the parties who are the principals in the suit must be avoided.[184]

Article V. The Promoter of Justice and the Defender of the Bond

Canon 1586 prescribes that the offices of promoter of justice and of defender of the bond shall be established in every diocese. The promoter of justice is a public official whose duties are the defense of the rights of the Church, through judicial procedure, in both contentious and criminal causes. The defender of the bond is likewise a public minister. To him is committed the defense of the bond of sacred ordination and of matrimony in trials and processes wherein that bond is impugned.[185] However, neither of these positions includes in itself any participation in the power of Orders or of jurisdiction, and therefore neither is an office in the strict sense.[186]

Both incumbents may be removed by the bishop through an act of simple removal, provided there is a just cause. The presence of such a cause seems requisite at least for the sake of licitness in the act of removal.[187] If the *officialis* had for a specific cause or trial constituted these priests in their positions, it seems that he would not be forbidden to remove them by means of an act of simple removal.[188] When they have been appointed permanently by the ordinary, they do not lose their office if the see becomes vacant, nor can they be removed by the vicar capitular or the diocesan administrator. However, as Dugan points out, if an apostolic administrator is permanently appointed over the diocese, he, inasmuch as he enjoys the rights and powers of a residential bishop, can recall the appointment of the promoter of justice and the defender of the bond.[189]

---

[184] Canon 1583: "Auditor in quovis litis momento ab officio removeri potest ab eo qui eundem elegit, iusta tamen de causa, et citra partium praeiudicium."

[185] Canon 1586; cf. Roberti, *De Processibus,* I, nn. 121, 124; Dugan, *op. cit.,* p. 65.

[186] Roberti, *op. cit.* n. 121; Coronata, *Institutiones,* III, 36; Cappello, *Summa Iuris Canonici,* III, 36.

[187] Canon 1590, § 2: "Iusta tamen intercedente causa, Episcopus eos removere potest." Cf. also Wernz-Vidal, VI, n. 117.

[188] Wernz-Vidal, *loc. cit.*

[189] Cf. Dugan, *op. cit.,* p. 72; canon 315, § 1.

Article VI. The Couriers and Apparitors

These officers act according to the order which comes to them from the judge. The courier, or messenger, may be employed for the purpose of conveying judicial information, e.g., a message from the court to one of the parties in litigation. The apparitor may be employed with a view to putting the sentences and decrees of the judge into execution.[190] Neither position connotes any participation in the power of Orders or of jurisdiction, as is clear from the fact that lay persons are to be appointed to these positions, unless in a particular case prudence dictates that clerics be called on to perform their functions.[191] Neither position therefore can be an office in the strict sense.

The removal of these officers follows the norms which, according to canon 373, regulate the removal of notaries.[192]

Article VII. The Diocesan Consultors

The position of diocesan consultors is created by the Code as a substitute for the office of canons of the cathedral chapter in those dioceses in which it has not yet been possible to institute or to revive the cathedral chapter.[193] It is true that the generic position of diocesan consultors has attached to it some participation on the power of jurisdiction, namely, in the rule of the diocese during the potential period of eight days subsequent to its vacancy, if the Holy See has made no contrary specific provision.[194] Nevertheless, it seems clear that whatever ordinary power is attached to this office by the Code is attached to the group or board of consultors as a unit rather than to the individual consultors. Hence, during the vacancy of the see it is the *board* of consultors which enjoys the ordinary power of ruling the diocese, and not any one individual consultor, until one of the members of the board be elected as the diocesan administrator, and thereupon rightfully rules in an individual capacity.[195]

---

[190] Canon 1591.

[191] Canon 1592; Cappello, *Summa Iuris Canonici,* III, 37.

[192] Canon 1592; cf. *supra,* p. 133.

[193] Canon 423.

[194] Cf. canons 427; 431, § 1; 435, § 1.

[195] Canon 435, § 1.

Canon 427 very definitely states that the *body* (*coetus*) of diocesan consultors takes the place of the cathedral chapter as the council of the bishop; wherefore whatever part in the government of the diocese the Code gives the cathedral chapter is also assigned to the body of consultors.[196] Accordingly it can hardly be maintained that the individual consultor has an office in the strict sense.

Diocesan consultors are not removable *ad nutum*. In order that they may be removed during the term of office, there must exist a just cause, and the previous advice of the other consultors must be obtained.[197] Decision as to what constitutes a just cause for removal is indeed left with the ordinary, but he is bound first to seek the advice of his other consultors. Absence of a just cause would not invalidate the act of removal, but would certainly make it illicit.[198] However, should the ordinary fail to take counsel with the other consultors, it seems, in the mind of the present writer, that in virtue of the ruling of canon 105, 1°,[199] the removal would be invalid.

The III Plenary Council of Baltimore (1884) listed some just causes for the removal of diocesan consultors: old age, infirmity and similar reasons by which the consultor has become unfit to perform his duties; or if he has rendered himself unworthy of his office by grave neglect, or by his own fault has suffered a notable loss of reputation.[200]

Since the consultors remain in office during the vacancy of the see,[201] the question may be asked whether the administrator of the vacant see can remove a consultor from office. Klekotka maintains that since the administrator is an ordinary, he can *per se* remove a consultor, but the author recommends that the administrator abstain from such action except when for some extraordinary

---

[196] ". . . de coetu quoque consultorum dioecesanorum intelligenda sunt."

[197] Canon 428: "Durante munere, consultores ne removeantur, nisi ob iustam causam ac de consilio ceterorum consultorum."

[198] Klekotka, *Diocesan Consultors,* The Catholic University of America Canon Law Studies, n. 8 (Washington, D. C.: The Catholic University of America, 1920), p. 92.

[199] ". . . si consilium exigatur tantum, per verba, ex. gr.: *de consilio consultorum,* vel *audito Capitulo, parocho,* etc., etc., satis est ad valide agendum ut Superior illas personas audiat."

[200] *Acta et Decreta,* n. 21.

[201] Canon 426, § 4.

reason the removal should become urgent. In other cases it is recommended that the undesirable consultor be urged to resign voluntarily, and thus leave the administrator free to appoint a new consultor.[202]

Article VIII. Ordinary and Extraordinary Confessors

The positions of ordinary and extraordinary confessor, which are generically established in the Code, are to be constituted for houses of lay religious, whether of men or of women,[203] for religious novitiates,[204] and for seminaries.[205] Both positions are conferred according to the norms of the common law, and both imply a participation in the power of jurisdiction for the one appointed. However, since obviously this power is a delegated one, these offices are ecclesiastical offices in the wide sense only.

Concerning the removal of the ordinary and extraordinary confessors of women religious, the Code is very explicit. The local ordinary may for a grave reason remove them even if the convent is subject to a regular superior and the confessor himself be a regular.[206] The local ordinary, who in this matter is the ordinary of the place where the religious house is situated,[207] is not bound to give any reason for the removal to anyone except the Holy See, when requested by it. If, however, the nuns are subject to a regular superior, the ordinary must notify that superior of the removal of the confessors.[208] For the removal of the confessors

[202] *Diocesan Consultors,* p. 93. Cappello holds that the administrator cannot remove the consultor except for some delict.—*Summa Iuris Canonici,* I, 435; cf. also Chelodi, *Ius de Personis,* n. 215.

[203] Canons 520, § 1; 521, § 1; 528.

[204] Canon 566.

[205] Canon 1361.

[206] This applies also to the special and supplementary confessors mentioned in canon 521, §§ 2, 3. Cf. Schaefer, *De Religiosis,* p. 391, footnote n. 236, where the author notes that a grave cause is not required for the removal of these confessors; Coronata, *Institutiones,* I, 687, footnote n. 3.

[207] Canon 876, § 2.

[208] Canon 527: "Loci Ordinarius, ad normam can. 880, potest, gravem ob causam, religiosarum confessarium tum ordinarium quam extraordinarium amovere, etiamsi monasterium regularibus subdatur et ipse sacerdos a confessionibus sit regularis, nec tenetur causam amotionis cuiquam significare, excepta Apostolica Sede, si ab ea requiratur; de amotione autem debet Superiorem regularem monere, si moniales regularibus subdantur."

during their term of office there is required a grave cause. In the absence of such a cause the ordinary would commit a grave sin were he to decree the removal.[209] However, a relatively grave cause, that is, relative to the external circumstances of time, place and persons, suffices.[210] Abuse of the sacrament, unsound doctrine, disturbance in the community, loss of good name on the part of the confessor—all these are sufficient reasons for the removal, although the causes need not necessarily connote guilt or sin on the side of the confessors.

If the nuns are subject to a regular superior, that superior cannot directly remove the confessors from their office. He can however revoke or suspend his permission for the hearing of confessions if the confessor is one of his own subjects, and in this manner indirectly prevent the confessor from exercising his office, except in the circumstances mentioned in canon 519.[211]

With regard to the same type of confessors for the lay religious houses of men, it may be argued from analogy with what has just been noted above that it is the local ordinary who is the competent superior to remove these confessors from office. For even in the lay religious institutes which are exempt, it is the local ordinary who delegates the jurisdiction of the confessors. The religious superior merely proposes the candidate for the office.[212] Here again, however, the superior can for a grave cause indirectly prevent the confessor from performing his office by revoking or suspending his permission, if said confessor is one of his own subjects.[213] It also seems but proper and in accordance with the spirit of the law that the local ordinary notify the religious superior of the removal of the confessor, just as he is required to do with regard to the removal of the ordinary and extraordinary confessors of women religious who are subject to a regular superior.[214]

Finally, with regard to the ordinary and extraordinary confessors of seminaries, there can be no doubt that it is the ordinary who is competent to remove the confessors.

---

[209] Coronata, *op. cit.*, I, 687.

[210] Schaefer, *op. cit.*, p. 392.

[211] Schaefer, *loc. cit.*

[212] Canon 875, § 2.

[213] Cf. canons 874, § 1; 880, § 1.

[214] Canon 527; cf. also *supra*, p. 90.

CHAPTER VI

The Requirements for the Act of Simple Removal From Office

Once it has been established who is the competent superior to decree the simple removal from office, and what incumbents of offices are subject to this type of removal, it remains to determine what is required by the law in order that the ordinary or superior may execute the removal.

Clerics, with the exclusion of pastors, who are removable in office can demand only the observance of the norms which have been established for their removal. It is true that the Code enacts certain specific requirements for the removal of the incumbents of such offices as the synodal examiners and parish priest consultors, the synodal judges, and the diocesan consultors.[1] However, such requirements are but restrictions which further particularize the general norm as enacted in canon 192, § 3. This canon deals with the removal from offices of incumbents who are removable apart from the necessary observance of any legal procedure.[2] For such clerics may be removed, even though they have committed no crime, for a just cause according to the prudent judgment of the ordinary, who in turn is obliged to see that the norms of natural equity are observed, such as the giving of due consideration to the good repute of the cleric, the according of deserved recognition for the past services rendered by him to the diocese, and the like,[3] and who must also duly intimate the fact of removal to the cleric whom he has removed from office.

---

[1] Cf. *supra*, pp. 133, 137, 143.

[2] ". . . privatio decerni ab Ordinario potest ex qualibet iusta causa, prudenti eius arbitrio, etiam citra delictum, naturali aequitate servata, sed certum procedendi modum sequi minime tenetur, salvo canonum praescripto circa paroecias amovibiles; privatio tamen effectum non habet, nisi postquam fuerit a superiore intimata."

[3] Cf. Augustine, *A Commentary on Canon Law,* II, 165.

SECTION I. THE REQUIREMENT OF A JUST CAUSE

Although the ordinary is not bound to follow any definite form of procedure in the matter of a removable incumbent's simple removal from his office, still the ordinary is definitely required to have a just cause before he proceeds to decree the removal of his priests from their offices. Even when the incumbents of the offices are removable *ad nutum,* there must exist some cause which in the mind of the ordinary justifies his action in a particular instance.[4] Such a demand is to be expected in an orderly society such as the Church. Arbitrariness, on the other hand, especially in such serious questions, is altogether foreign to the spirit of the Church and its law's solicitude for fairness.[5]

Since the Code does not supply any list of specific causes, it is necessary for the ordinary to form his own judgment concerning the justice of the cause in each individual case. To this purpose let the ordinary heed the advice given by the Council of Trent that bishops should remember that they are shepherds, and consequently they should love their subjects as children and brethren in Christ. Let him balance with this the poignant theme of the decree *Maxima cura: "Salus enim populi suprema lex."*[6] On the basis of this any reason or cause which satisfies the prudent judgment of the ordinary is sufficient to justify the removal.[7]

Any arbitrariness, whim, or mere personal grievance on the part of the ordinary is entirely out of place. Moreover, since ecclesiastical offices vary in dignity and importance, it seems logical that the just cause will vary in the same proportion. The more important the office is, the more grave also should be the cause which will permit the removal from that office.[8] Again, a more grave cause may be required for the removal from a specific office because of the circumstances, as, for example, when the present incumbent is the only person capable of fulfilling the duties of the office under

---

[4] Cf. *supra,* p. 86.

[5] *ASS,* III (1867), 510-511; cf. *supra,* p. 41.

[6] S.C. Consist., decr. *Maxima cura,* 20 aug. 1910, Proemium—*AAS,* II (1910), 636.

[7] Cf. canon 2299, § 1, as a parallel canon.

[8] Thus, e.g., Wernz demands a grave cause for the removal of the vicar general.—*Ius Decretalium,* II, tit. XXXVII, n. 806.

consideration. In general, the cause may have reference to the good of the Church, to the good of souls, or to the good of the incumbent himself.[9] It is worthy of note also that the cause may have reference to a temporal good as well as to a spiritual one.[10]

Despite the fact that the requirement of a just cause must be considered as of great importance, it must be admitted that it is not necessary for the validity of the removal in the present law. Canon 192, § 3, is not so worded as to incorporate the elements which are necessary if a law is to be considered as an invalidating law.[11] As far, then, as the general norm of this canon is concerned, a just cause is required only for the lawfulness of the act of removal.

Still the question may be asked: what would constitute a just cause for a simple removal from office? As a guide or norm with which to form a prudent judgment in this matter, the ordinary can do well to consider the various causes which the Code gives concerning the penal and administrative removals from office. Simple removal is concerned primarily with removal aside from any delict or fault on the part of the incumbent. Nevertheless, if the law permits the ordinary to remove a removable incumbent from office for any just cause, then surely the ordinary can be guided somewhat in his determination of the justice of that cause in a given case by the reasons given in the Code itself with regard to the other types of removal, or even privation in the strict sense. For, even though canon 192, § 3, uses the phrase *"etiam citra delictum,"* it cannot be said to exclude entirely cases wherein a crime or wrongdoing has been committed or is suspected, or wherein there exists a cause which, aside from any grave fault, renders the ministry of the cleric harmful or at least ineffective.[12]

---

[9] Cf. Ayrinhac, *Constitution of the Church in the New Code of Canon Law,* p. 365; Zaplotnik, *De Vicariis Foraneis,* p. 64.

[10] Cf. Zaplotnik, *loc. cit.;* also *supra,* p. 89.

[11] Canon 11: "Irritantes aut inhabilitantes eae tantum leges habendae sunt, quibus aut actum esse nullum aut inhabilem esse personam expresse vel aequivalenter statuitur."

[12] Cf., e.g., canon 2147, concerning the removal of pastors. It would be beyond the purpose of the present work to give any lengthy commentary on these causes. For a fuller treatment of their direct application to the administrative removal of pastors the reader is again referred to the often cited work of Connor, *The Administrative Removal of Pastors.*

Thus in the analytical index of the Code under the term *"privatio"* may be found the following causes for which the ordinary *shall* deprive a cleric of his office: 1) if a cleric is an apostate or falls into heresy or schism and, after a warning, does not repent;[13] 2) if a canon penitentiary is gravely neglectful in the duties of his office, and after admonitions persists in this neglect for over a year and a half;[14] 3) if a cleric who is actually living in concubinage, or even suspected thereof, has failed to obey the precept of his bishop or to answer the ordinary, and has not amended within eight months from the time the bishop has suspended him;[15] 4) if a cleric in major orders has committed an offense against the sixth commandment with minors under sixteen years of age, or has been guilty of adultery, of rape, of bestiality, of sodomy, of pandering, or of incest, or has sinned against the sixth commandment even in other ways;[16] 5) if a cleric has conspired against the authority of the Roman Pontiff or his legates, or his own proper ordinary, or against their legitimate commands, and also if a cleric has provoked subjects to disobedience towards them;[17] 6) if a cleric has been legitimately declared guilty of homicide, of usury, of robbery, or of theft in a very grave matter;[18] 7) if a cleric has obstinately remained under suspension for six months, and then, after admonitions, has not abandoned his obstinacy after the lapse of a month;[19] 8) if a priest has committed the crime of solicitation as mentioned in canon 904;[20] 9) if a cleric who has an office with the care of souls has attempted suicide;[21] 10) if a cleric, either in person or through orders, has presumptuously converted to his own use and usurped ecclesiastical goods of any kind, whether personal or real, or has prevented those to whom such goods rightfully belong from receiving the income deriving from

[13] Canon 2314, § 1, n. 2.

[14] Canon 2384.

[15] Cf. canons 2176; 2177, 3°; 2180; 2181; 2359, § 1.

[16] Canon 2359, §§ 2, 3.

[17] Canon 2331, § 2.

[18] Canon 2354, § 2.

[19] Canon 2340, § 2.

[20] Canon 2368, § 1.

[21] Canon 2350, § 2.

these goods;[22] and 11) if a cleric who holds an office to which the obligation of residence is attached has unlawfully absented himself.[23]

The ordinary *can* deprive a cleric of his office: 1) if a cleric has forged or falsified letters, decrees or rescripts of the Apostolic See, or with full knowledge of the forgery has made use of the letters, decrees or rescripts;[24] 2) if a cleric has inflicted injury upon another by words or writings or in any other manner, or has damaged the good reputation of another;[25] 3) if a cleric has carried on traffic in Mass stipends, etc., contrary to the precepts of canons 827, 828, and 840, § 1;[26] 4) if a cleric has taken away, destroyed, hidden or substantially altered, either personally or through the agency of others, any documents pertaining to the episcopal curia;[27] 5) if a cleric, in violation of canon 1406, stubbornly persists in his refusal to make the profession of faith;[28] and 6) if a cleric directly or indirectly has impeded the exercise of ecclesiastical jurisdiction, and has had recourse for that end to any lay authority, or if he has joined the Masons or other associations of the same kind.[29]

It must be remembered that all the causes just enumerated presuppose crime or guilt on the part of the cleric, and consequently are properly referrable to privation in the strict sense. For these delicts are specifically mentioned in the law as furnishing ground for a privation of office by way of vindictive penalty. The penalty is to be inflicted in a judicial manner if the incumbent is irremovable. If, however, he is removable, then it may be inflicted in a judicial manner or simply by means of a decree of privation. Nevertheless these causes certainly suffice for the act of simple removal from office. While these causes are indeed more properly

[22] Canon 2346.

[23] Canon 2381, § 2; cf. canons 2168-2175.

[24] Canon 2360, § 2.

[25] Canon 2355.

[26] Canon 2324.

[27] Canon 2405. By analogy, if a priest falsified or forged documents in the parish registries, there would be ample cause for invoking the act of simple removal, e.g., of an assistant pastor.

[28] Canon 2403.

[29] Canon 2336, §§ 1, 2.

linked with the concept of privation, yet they serve as apt examples for determining the justice of a cause relative also to the act of simple removal from office.

More to the point, perhaps, are the causes which the Code lists in relation to the administrative removal of pastors, as indicated in canon 2147. These causes suffice for the execution of a removal from office even aside from any grave fault on the part of the pastor, and, therefore, may serve as norms with reference to the act of simple removal from office.[30]

The legislator enunciates the general principle that a pastor can be removed for a cause which renders his ministry harmful or at least ineffective.[31] He then goes on to enumerate some particular causes in which the principle is verified. It will be to the purpose of the present work to consider each of these causes in brief, and to relate them to the offices whose incumbents are removable by means of an act of simple removal.

A—Incompetence. It goes without saying that any cleric who holds an ecclesiastical office must know at least what is necessary for the proper discharge of his duties. Moreover the Code itself demands higher learning for some offices, for example, the offices of vicar general,[32] diocesan consultors,[33] and *officialis*.[34] The extent of the information and learning that is required is, then, relative to the peculiar needs of the office.[35] Should a priest be found wanting in the necessary knowledge for the office he is now holding, then there is cause for his removal.

Knowledge or learning, however, is not the only requirement. Another most important one is good judgment. If a priest lacks that quality, then there is surely cause for his removal from office. Moreover, while incompetence to be a canonical cause for the

---

[30] Augustine, *A Commentary on Canon Law,* II, 165; Schaefer, *De Religiosis,* p. 921.

[31] Canon 2147, § 1: "Parochus . . . amoveri potest ob causam, quae ipsius ministerium, etiam citra gravem suam culpam, noxium aut saltem inefficax reddit."

[32] Canon 367, § 1.

[33] Canon 423.

[34] Canon 1573, § 4.

[35] Cf. Connor, *The Administrative Removal of Pastors,* p. 53.

removal of a pastor must be permanent,[36] even temporary incompetence would suffice as a cause for a simple removal from office.

B—Mental Infirmity. The phrase *infirmitas mentis* is quite comprehensive. It embraces all physical disorders that are many and varied, for example, imbecility, which may result from a serious illness or from old age and which impairs the power of judgment. For a simple removal it seems that even a temporary mental infirmity would justify the incumbent's removal, if the good of the Church and of souls were impaired by this weakness. However, a brief illness which might cause some mental disturbance at the time hardly seems to furnish a sufficient cause for the incumbent's removal, when it can be foreseen that the priest will soon be normal again and able to resume his duties. The ultimate decision of course rests with the ordinary.

C—Bodily Infirmity. A priest may also be removed from office for bodily infirmity, provided that he is incapacitated or seriously hindered in the due performance of his duties. Paralysis, serious stammering, deafness and blindness are some of the maladies and impairments mentioned by the authors.[37] To these may be added old age in so far as that hinders the incumbent in the fulfillment of the duties proper to his office. In all of these matters of course much will depend on the extent of the disease, the nature of the office which the cleric possesses, and finally the prudent judgment of the ordinary that the position cannot be adequately carried on unless the present incapacitated incumbent is removed.

D—Animosity of the People. The animosity of the people, even though unjust and not universal, is also a sufficient cause for the incumbent's removal, provided it is such as to hinder a priest from exercising a successful ministry, and is not expected to abate soon. The phrase *odium plebis* means more than mere indifference or antipathy.[38] This animosity may express itself in insults and demonstrations against the priest, but such manifestations are not essential to the concept.[39] It consists then in a positive

---

[36] Connor, *op. cit.*, p. 54; cf. also canon 475.

[37] Cf. Connor, *op. cit.*, p. 58.

[38] Augustine, *A Commentary on Canon Law,* VII, 416.

[39] Connor, *The Administrative Removal of Pastors,* p. 61.

hostility of the people against a priest to the extent that they neglect or refuse his ministrations.

It could happen that the priest does not get along well in his particular office with his fellow priests. Just to what extent this animosity, whether it comes from the laity or the clergy, proves an obstacle to the good of the Church and of souls will have to be judged by the ordinary from the circumstances of each case. If the animosity is deserved because the priest himself was responsible, then the way would be clear for his removal. If however it is unjust, then the ordinary should do his utmost to remove the cause of the animosity rather than to remove the incumbent from the office.[40]

E—Loss of Esteem. Another cause sufficient for an incumbent's removal is the loss of the priest's good reputation among virtuous and serious-minded persons, whether it arises from his frivolous conduct or from a former crime which has recently been detected, and for which he cannot now be punished inasmuch as legitimate prescription has run its full course, or from the conduct of members of his household or of blood-relations living with him, unless by their departure the good name of the priest can be restored.

It goes without saying that if a man's reputation is among his most priceless possessions, a priest's reputation is still more important by reason of his priesthood, no matter what specific office in the Church he may hold. Of course the higher the office, the greater the need for the preservation of that good name. Any loss of that esteem must have resulted, not among gossipers, but among persons of honesty and integrity and such as see things in their proper light.[41]

A priest may lose his good reputation because of his levity of conduct. Once his outward behavior savors of levity or frivolity, even by simple neglect or omission, he is liable to suspicion and may lose the esteem of the people. Even though he is not guilty of any external, or at least public, mortal sin, he can nevertheless suffer that loss of esteem which will hinder his work in the spe-

---

[40] Cf. Connor, *op. cit.*, p. 64.

[41] Connor, *op. cit.*, p. 65.

cific office he holds, and thus his removal from that office would be justified.[42]

Loss of reputation may also come from a priest's former occult crime which has become a matter of common knowledge. By reason of the intervening legitimate prescription[43] this crime can no longer be punished judicially. But since it has now become publicly known with scandal to the people, and a consequent loss of reputation to the priest, there is sufficient cause for his removal from office.

Finally, the conduct of a member of a priest's household or of a relative living with him may be such as to cause a loss of reputation to the priest. If such conduct, whether sinful or not, renders the priest's ministry harmful or worthless, then there is cause for his removal, unless by their departure the good reputation of the priest can be restored. However, as Connor wisely observes, the temper of people in these matters varies in different localities.[44] What would create a serious scandal in one locality may occasion little comment in another. The final judgment rests with the ordinary.

F—Probable Occult Crime. A priest may also be removed from office whenever there is probability that he has committed an occult crime, which, as the ordinary prudently foresees, will in the future become a source of scandal.[45] Prudence demands that the ordinary foresee that the probable occult crime will become a matter of public knowledge. For if it remains occult, there can be no scandal. Moreover, the ordinary should have more than a mere suspicion of a priest's occult crime before he resorts to the act of his removal from office. He should carefully weigh the nature and circumstances of the alleged crime, the number, character and motives of the informants, and the previous record of the priest.

G—Inefficient Administration of Temporal Affairs. While this cause for an incumbent's removal from office, as it is mentioned in the Code, has special application to pastors and to the adminis-

---

[42] Connor, *op. cit.*, p. 66.

[43] Cf. canons 1701-1705.

[44] *The Administrative Removal of Pastors*, p. 70.

[45] Cf. canon 2197, 4°, for the meaning of an occult crime.

trative removal of the same, still it may be applied to other clerics insofar as they administer church property, especially pastors who belong to a religious community and who are removable *ad nutum.* Hence, if a cleric is negligent in his observance of the rules of canon law concerning the temporal goods of the church, there would exist a sufficient cause for his removal from office.[46]

Whether or not moral guilt be present, if a priest has failed in these matters to the extent that direct harm is done to the temporal good of the Church, and indirect harm to the good of souls, then certainly the ordinary has a just cause for the priest's removal from his office. Furthermore, as Connor observes, it is not demanded that this harm has already occurred; moral certainty that it will occur suffices.[47]

It seems warranted to include here also a list of causes which have special reference to the jurisdiction of the local ordinary over religious communities in his territory. These will serve as a guide in the determination of the reasonableness of the cause for the removal of pastors who belong to a religious community. For such pastors are removable simply at the will of the local ordinary or of their own proper superior.[48] Nevertheless both the local ordinary and the superior must have a just cause before either resorts to the removal of the pastor.

A sufficient or just cause for removal would exist: 1) when the religious refuses submission and obedience to the vicar or the prefect apostolic in those things in which the Code subjects the religious to his authority;[49] 2) when the laws concerning the subjection of religious pastors to local ordinaries are not observed, as for example, the regulations concerning the duration of a pastor's permissible absence from his parish;[50] 3) when the prescriptions of the local ordinary are not observed in regard to money received for the parishes or the missions;[51] 4) when the

---

[46] Cf., e.g., canons 1522; 1525; 1526; 1281, § 1; 1539, § 1; 1532; 1537; 1545.

[47] *The Administrative Removal of Pastors,* p. 79; cf. Sipos, *Enchiridion Iuris Canonici,* p. 911.

[48] Cf. canon 454, § 5.

[49] Canons 295-298; 307.

[50] Cf. canons 451, § 1; 454, § 5; 465, §§ 4, 5; 630; 631, §§ 1, 2.

[51] Canon 533, § 1, 4°.

safeguards for divine worship and for the integrity of morals as prescribed by the local ordinary are not observed;[52] 5) when they refuse to comply with the enactments of the local ordinary concerning the ringing of bells, or the recitation of public prayers;[53] 6) when the rights of the ordinary concerning the consecration or blessing of exempt places in his territory are denied him;[54] 7) when prayers and exercises of piety are conducted in opposition to the regulations enacted by the local ordinary;[55] 8) when rules made to govern Benediction of the Blessed Sacrament are deliberately ignored;[56] 9) when a reasonable request of the local ordinary concerning assistance in matters of catechetical and religious instruction is refused;[57] and 10) when legitimate contributions for the diocesan seminary are withheld, as also for other extraordinary diocesan assessments.[58]

In addition to the causes just enumerated at length in the present chapter, many others could be listed as examples of sufficient reasons for the effecting of a simple removal from office. Many of these have been mentioned in the preceding chapter in connection with the various offices whose incumbents are subject to a simple removal from their office. The cause, it must be noted, need not be one which is associated with a failing or with negligence on the part of the incumbent. There can exist other positive reasons which justify the incumbent's removal in given circumstances, provided of course that equity be duly observed.

So, for example, the ordinary may wish to promote the incumbent of an office to a higher position or to one where he is needed because of his ability, etc. Again, the ordinary may wish to relieve a priest of duties which the bishop feels are a burden to the priest or entail an impairing of his health. Finally, he may wish to train other priests in a particular position, such as in the chancery office. The future good of the diocese may demand such a policy.

---

[52] Canon 1261, § 2.

[53] Canon 612.

[54] Canons 1155, § 1; 1157; 1169.

[55] Canon 1259, § 1.

[56] Canon 1274, § 1.

[57] Canons 1334; 1336.

[58] Canons 1355; 1356; 1505.

The ultimate decision as to the reasonableness of the cause rests of course with the ordinary or the proper superior, and not with the incumbent who is to be removed. If the priest feels that he has been wronged, then he still has an available means of redress, namely recourse to the Holy See against the decree of removal.

SECTION II. THE OBSERVANCE OF NATURAL EQUITY

No matter how just the cause for removal may be, unless at the same time natural equity is preserved, the removal may not lawfully take place. This is an inescapable conclusion from canon 192, § 3, itself.[59] Should the ordinary, in disregard of this requirement, remove a cleric from office, there is then a basis for a recourse to the Holy See. What then is the meaning of the phrase *"naturali aequitate servata"* in canon 192, § 3?

In general, the term *aequitas* which is translated into English by the word equity sometimes signifies natural justice, at other times an ideal law or norm, at other times a proper moderation, and even at times *epikeia*. Even in the Code itself this term, which occurs six times, is used with some difference of meaning, though the fundamental idea in most instances is the same.[60] However, it is the term as an ablative absolute with the adjective *"naturali"* and the participle *"servata,"* as found in canons 144 and 192, § 3, with which the present work is concerned. For only in these two canons is the term used in exactly the same way, conveying exactly the same idea.[61]

Natural equity, as applied in these canons, may be defined: a corrective element of law by which an ecclesiastical judge (or superior), in view of a spiritual good, common or private, applies justice in concrete cases either by tempering or aggravating the existing norms.[62] This equity has as its foundation, or basic root,

[59] ". . . ex qualibet iusta causa . . . naturali aequitate servata." Cf. Toso, *Ad Codicem Iuris Canonici . . . Commentaria Minora* (5 vols., Romae: Marietti, 1920-1927), II, 111 (hereafter cited as *Commentaria Minora*).

[60] Cf. canons 20; 144; 192, § 3; 643, § 2; 1455, 2° and 1833, 2°.

[61] Cf. Roelker, "The Meaning of 'Aequitas,' 'Aequus' and 'Aeque' in the Code of Canon Law"—*The Jurist,* VI (1946), 239-274.

[62] Cf. d'Angelo, "De Aequitate in Codice Iuris Canonici,"—*Apollinaris* (Romae: Apud Aedes Facultatis Iuridicae, 1928-), I (1928), 373.

the virtue of justice, and therefore the question involved is one of strict rights under law in virtue of the possession of an office or its equivalent.[63]

It is called natural, so d'Angelo (1885-1930) stated,[64] because it must be established by the judge (or ordinary) himself, and its ultimate determination and application is left to his prudent judgment. It is therefore a subjective element of law which the superior applies to a given case (in the present consideration to the removal from office) to insure justice and fairness in the application of an already existing norm of law. Whether it is a question of tempering the law, or of heightening its application in a given case, will depend upon the circumstances.[65] Either alternative is possible, but in both the rights of the person affected, that is, of the cleric who is removed from office, must be respected and safeguarded, otherwise equity will be violated. In other words, whenever the ordinary makes use of the power given him in canon 192, § 3, he has a grave obligation to see to it that the rights in equity of the cleric to be removed from office do not suffer beyond what is deserved.

Since canon 192, § 3, does not offer any suggestion or indicate any method whereby equity can be recognized and respected, it is difficult at times to determine exactly what would be equitable. Hence it rests with the ordinary to determine what he considers a sufficient recompense for the loss of an office. But it must be kept in mind that the equity indicated in canon 192, § 3, embraces more than the preservation of the rights which arise from one's title of ordination. For that is fundamental justice and a clearly indicated obligation in virtue of canon 981, § 2.[66]

Equity in the matter of removal from office is founded, not on the title of ordination, but on the possession of an office, and therefore it is a question, not merely of a cleric's support, but also of

---

[63] Roelker, *"art. cit."—The Jurist,* VI (1946), 242.

[64] *"Art. cit."—Apollinaris,* I (1928), 372.

[65] Cf. canons 2221-2222; d'Angelo, *ibid.,* p. 373.

[66] "Ordinarius presbytero, quem promoverit titulo servitii ecclesiae vel missionis, debet beneficium vel officium vel subsidium, ad congruam eiusdem sustentationem sufficiens, conferre."

a compensation for what has been sacrificed.[67] Any removal without at least the adequate support owed a cleric in virtue of his title of ordination is certainly contrary to the spirit of canon 192, § 3, and a violation of justice. But equity here goes beyond that minimum, and that too not by reason of charity or mercy. Even when the office is one whose incumbent is removable *ad nutum,* for example, the office of the vicar general, the *officialis,* the religious pastors mentioned in canon 454, § 5, the parochial vicars mentioned in canons 472-476, and the vicars forane, this observance of equity is necessary, otherwise the ordinary acts unlawfully.[68]

When a cleric has been guilty of crime, obviously his rights in equity suffer. Nevertheless the ordinary must be careful that the cleric be not made to suffer beyond what he has deserved. Privation of office may be punishment enough.[69] Should the ordinary deprive of his office a cleric who has been guilty of some crime, and then bestow upon him an office of inferior worth, that cleric could hardly claim a violation of equity. But in no case wherein the law does not permit the loss of sustenance which is derived from the title of ordination is a cleric to be punished with that loss. Thus the penalty of deposition, which includes such a loss,[70] is in no way involved in the normal operation of canon 192, § 3. As Roelker insists, equity is undoubtedly violated when undue punishments are inflicted.[71]

When, on the other hand, there has been no crime, and the question of a simple removal from office arises, the ordinary must take special care to insure the observance of natural equity. For the cleric should not suffer more than his removal entails. Hence, if possible, there should be a suitable exchange of offices, or at least an adequate compensation for the loss incurred. It seems scarcely equitable, for example, to remove a priest from his office,

---

[67] Roelker, *ibid.,* p. 242.

[68] Cf. Cappello, *Summa Iuris Canonici,* I, 350, 437; Chelodi, *Ius de Personis,* nn. 200, 222; Vermeersch-Creusen, *Epitome,* I, n. 483; Zaplotnik, *De Vicariis Foraneis,* p. 64.

[69] Roelker, *ibid.,* p. 243.

[70] Cf. canon 2303.

[71] *Loc. cit.*

even from the office of assistant pastor, and send him to a university for further studies without adequate compensation and with only the minimum of sustenance. Of course, in line with the spirit of sacrifice demanded by the priesthood, it is expected that occasionally a priest will suffer some loss as a result of his removal from office. As long as this loss is not beyond what would be expected, the question of the violation of natural equity does not arise. The presumption is that the ordinary is operating honestly and prudently according to law. When, however, that loss exceeds what can be considered normal, the question of the violation of equity definitely does arise.[72]

If the cleric who has been removed feels that his rights in equity have been violated, he can have recourse to the Holy See. But as a priest he should be willing to make normal sacrifices, especially when, for example, his removal from one office and his appointment to another, even though a lower one, is occasioned by the needs of the diocese, the good of souls, etc. So the bishop may wish to remove a priest from one office in order that the priest may devote his talents for the good of the diocese in some other office, which can be best served by this particular priest. As long as the good reputation or honor of the priest does not suffer by such a removal and subsequent appointment to an inferior office, it seems that there would be no violation of equity.

Further light is shed on the question of natural equity as indicated in canon 192, § 3, from the recommendations offered by the authors. Blat makes the general statement that reason should dictate what is to be done.[73] Cappello,[74] Cocchi,[75] Ojetti (1862-1932),[76] Chelodi (1880-1922),[77] and Berutti[78] demand that caution be used lest the reputation or good name of the incumbent suffer by reason of the removal, especially when there has been no

---

[72] Roelker, *Art. cit.—The Jurist,* VI (1946), 243-244.

[73] *Commentarium,* II, 160.

[74] *Summa Iuris Canonici,* I, 350, 437.

[75] *Commentarium,* Lib. II, pars. I, n. 106.

[76] *Commentarium in Codicem Iuris Canonici* (4 vols., Romae: Apud Aedes Universitatis Gregorianae, 1927-1931), II, 176.

[77] *Ius de Personis,* n. 149.

[78] *Institutiones,* II, 302.

crime. Ojetti insisted further that the removal be made carefully so that no notable damage or loss in financial matters be incurred by the cleric, and his support be put in jeopardy.[79] Cocchi,[80] De Meester,[81] Chelodi[82] and Berutti[83] also support this statement. Coronata, moreover, maintains that a removal from office is not to bring dishonor to a cleric, even though he be an incumbent who is removable *ad nutum*.[84] All of these matters must be weighed conscientiously by the ordinary before he decrees the removal. To help in his determination he can do well to keep in mind the recommendation of Augustine that merit and previous service to the diocese be taken into consideration.[85]

All the foregoing statements clearly indicate that the opinion of Maroto (1875-1937) cannot be held. For he implied that nothing is due a cleric who aside from the consideration of crime has been removed from his office, provided that the right to support as arising from his title of ordination is safe.[86]

By analogy with the law regarding the provision for dispossessed pastors, as indicated in canon 2154, § 1, the ordinary can obtain a further guide to be followed for the act of simple removal from office. That canon directs that, according to the facts and circumstances of the case, the pastor who has been removed may be either transferred to another parish, assigned to some other office or benefice if he is capable, or pensioned.[87] It cannot be insisted or even suggested that this law must be applied as such to the question of a simple removal from office. But it can be suggested that this law be kept in mind by the ordinary as a guide by which he can better recognize and determine natural equity.[88]

---

[79] *Loc. cit.*

[80] *Loc. cit.*

[81] *Compendium,* I, 299.

[82] *Loc. cit.*

[83] *Loc. cit.*

[84] *Institutiones,* I, 502.

[85] *A Commentary on Canon Law,* II, 165.

[86] *Institutiones,* I, 817.

[87] ". . . vel assignatione alius officii aut beneficii, si ad haec idoneus sit, sive pensione."

[88] For a further development of the law of canon 2154, the reader is referred to Connor, *The Administrative Removal of Pastors,* pp. 125-137.

At any rate, it is for the ordinary, not for the cleric himself, to determine the form which the cleric's provision is to take.

SECTION III. NOTIFICATION REGARDING THE REMOVAL

Once it is clear that there is present a just and reasonable cause for removal, and that the demands of equity have been satisfied, the ordinary or the superior must see to it that proper notification of the removal is made to the incumbent to be removed. Without this due notification, the removal has no effect, as is evident from canon 192, § 3.[89]

The Code indeed gives no indication as to the manner in which the notification is to be made. It seems clear, however, that if the removal, or rather, the privation, is made in a judicial manner, then the notification is achieved by the sentence of the judge. If, on the other hand, there is question of merely a simple removal, then notification can be made by a decree of the ordinary.[90] For the ordinary's decisions in matters subject to his executive and administrative powers are usually formulated as decrees.

The common law does not require that the notification be made in writing or orally before two witnesses in order to be effective. However, if the ordinary wishes to remove an incumbent from office, he has to make the fact formally known to him, for a tacit recall or removal is not valid, nor does it affect the validity of the continued acts of the incumbent.[91] The notification may be made orally by the ordinary himself, or through some official of the curia, but the ordinary must assure himself of the fact that the notice was received. As Augustine maintained, the best way is in writing, although this mode is not strictly involved in the term

---

Special attention is called to that author's statement that the obligation of the ordinary to provide for the future of a pastor who has been removed depends to a great extent on circumstances. It is governed, for example, by the pastor's previous record, his age, health, mental ability, etc.—*Op. cit.*, p. 125.

[89] ". . . privatio tamen effectum non habet, nisi postquam fuerit a Superiore intimata."

[90] Toso, *Commentaria Minora*, II, 160.

[91] Cf. Augustine, *A Commentary on Canon Law*, II, 405.

"intimata," which simply connotes that something be made known to someone in a legal way.[92]

Some analogy also may be invoked with the law concerning the notification of the superior's acceptance of the resignation of an office, as indicated in canon 190, §§ 1, 2.[93] Hence it follows that the incumbent remains in his office until he receives the notification, howsoever it is made, of the superior's act of removal. Although one may not demand an authentic written document, nevertheless the importance of the notification dictates that care should be taken that the party to be removed certainly receives it.[94]

From a practical viewpoint it may be observed that, unless care is taken in this matter, there is danger that the ordinary may confer an office before it is actually vacant. For, in virtue of canon 150, § 1, such a conferral is invalid, and the subsequent vacancy does not rectify the matter.[95] To avoid inconveniences and confusion which can arise from such an action, the ordinary must take proper precautions to guarantee that the notification of removal arrives at its destination.

Finally, it may be noted that if the ordinary should withdraw his act of removal before it has been intimated to the incumbent, it follows that the incumbent would retain the office by reason of the former title.

---

[92] *Loc. cit.*

[93] "Officium, renuntiatione legitime facta et acceptata, vacat postquam renuntianti significata est acceptatio."

"Renuntians in officio permaneat donec de Superioris acceptatione certum nuntium acceperit." Cf. Berutti, *Institutiones,* II, 295, 302.

[94] Cf. McDevitt, *The Renunciation of an Ecclesiastical Office,* p. 109.

[95] "Provisio officii de iure non vacantis ad normam can. 183, § 1, est ipso facto irrita, nec subsequente vacatione convalescit."

CHAPTER VII

Recourse to the Holy See

The Church has always stressed the fact that the Holy See is a haven of protection for the faithful, both the clergy and the laity. Over it rules the Vicar of Christ, whom they may approach not only for guidance, but even for defense against unjust actions. Accordingly against the decree of a simple removal from office the law affords a remedy or a means of redress for the one who claims that he has suffered injury in his rights by such a removal.[1] This remedy is known as recourse, a general remedy which may be employed against any extrajudicial act of an ordinary.[2] Some explanation then must be given concerning the meaning of the recourse, the manner of making it, the superior to whom it is made, and finally its effect—all with a particular application to the question of the simple removal from office.

SECTION I. THE MEANING OF THE RECOURSE

In general, recourse as a juridical means of redress may be defined as "a plea made to a competent superior with a view to its possible unfavorable reflection upon the extrajudicial acts of a lesser superior, inasmuch as the one who presents the plea either claims or at least opines that he has suffered injury in his rights or detriment in his status."[3]

---

[1] Canon 192, § 3: ". . . et ab Ordinarii decreto datur recursus ad Sedem Apostolicam, sed in devolutivo tantum." Cf. also canon 454, § 5.

[2] Beste, *Introductio in Codicem,* p. 267.

[3] McClunn, *Administrative Recourse,* The Catholic University of America Canon Law Studies, n. 240 (Washington, D. C.: The Catholic University of America Press, 1946), p. 11; ". . . quo apud superiorem altioris gradus contra suum ordinarium conqueritur in ordine ad obtinendam correctionem, emendationem vel etiam revocationem ordinationis sibi adversae. Talis provocatio . . . proprie nomine a Codice insignitur 'recursus,' si interponatur contra dispositiones administrativas seu provisiones extraiudiciales . . ."—Beste, *Introductio in Codicem,* p. 773.

Recourse differs from appeal. The latter is the ordinary means available against possible violations of one's rights through sentences pronounced by the judicial authorities in the Church.[4] Recourse, however, is the extrajudicial counterpart of appeal, and is the remedy established by positive ecclesiastical law against the extrajudicial or administrative acts, decrees, etc., of superiors.[5] Recourse, too, need not always be concerned with a strict right, but may deal with the interest or the concern of the party. Thus the Code makes it clear that the local ordinary has no strict right to prevent the religious superior from removing a religious pastor from office; yet the ordinary can have a recourse in this matter.[6]

A question that may be asked is the following: May one make this recourse to the Holy See against a decree of removal effected by a person who functions with a vicarious ordinary power? In other words, posited the fact that a vicar general has this power and has issued a decree of removal, must that action stand confirmed by the bishop before a recourse to Rome is possible in the case? There is nothing in the law to impede the use of recourse in such a case. But, as McClunn suggests, the more expeditious and practical method of reaching a solution would be to present the matter to the bishop for a review. This step is simply the presentation of a plea for a rehearing of the facts in the case by the same juridical authority. If the bishop revokes the action of his vicar general, then the plea has achieved its desired end; if, however, he confirms the vicar's action, then the way for a recourse to the Holy See is still open.[7]

SECTION II. THE MANNER OF MAKING THE RECOURSE

While it is necessary that a judicial appeal be initiated before the judge against whose sentence the redress is sought,[8] the Code is generally silent on the procedure for recourse. McClunn con-

[4] Canon 1879. Thus if a cleric is deprived of his office in a judicial manner by the sentence of a judge, his means of redress is not recourse, but appeal. Cf. Beste, *op. cit.*, p. 926.

[5] McClunn, *Administrative Recourse,* p. 12.

[6] Cf. canon 454, § 5; *supra,* p. 105.

[7] *Administrative Recourse,* p. 30.

[8] Canon 1881.

cludes that there is no need of interposing the recourse before the ordinary against whom the redress is sought.[9] But the recourse is made simply by forwarding to the Holy See the petition in the form of a letter.[10]

This letter should be typewritten, or at least written in a legible style in one of the languages of the Roman Curia, viz., Latin, French or Italian. It should be brief, clear, and to the point. It should give only what is necessary for a proper understanding of the point on which the recourse insists. Thus it should contain the name of the petitioner, of his place of residence, and of his diocese or religious community; the matter of the recourse should be given, that is, the removal from office; the decree of removal should be stated together with the name, office, and residence of the ordinary who gave the decree. Finally, the reasons for the recourse should be stated completely with a view to showing why the petitioner regards the decree of removal as unjust and injurious, for example, for the lack of a just case, or in consequence of the failure to observe natural equity, or at least why the petitioner considered the removal detrimental to his rights or interests. The date should be affixed and the letter signed by the party making the recourse.[11]

In the event that an incumbent who has been removed from office wishes to make use of this means of redress, must he notify the ordinary or the superior that a recourse has been made? Obviously there is no need of obtaining the permission of the ordinary to make the recourse, as the Code clearly gives all necessary permission in canon 192, § 3. When, moreover, this recourse is without a suspensive effect, as it is in canon 192, § 3, there is no reason for demanding even that the ordinary be notified that recourse has been made, since his jurisdiction in the matter of simple removal remains unhampered despite the recourse.[12]

---

[9] *Op. cit.*, pp. 36-37.

[10] Cf. McClunn, *op. cit.*, p. 37, where the author refers to the teaching of Wernz-Vidal that the custom of the Sacred Congregations is to decline the admission of oral petitions; and, in the same place, where he refers to a letter of the Papal Secretary of State forbidding the sending of petitions by telegraph.

[11] Cf. McClunn, *Administrative Recourse*, pp. 41-43.

[12] Cf. McClunn, *op. cit.*, p. 38.

Though not required either for validity or for licitness, such a notification is certainly advisable, if for no other reason than for a speedy outcome of the request. The Holy See will hardly revoke the ordinary's decree without hearing his views on the matter. If the ordinary or the superior knows of the proposed recourse, then he may forward to Rome a statement of his views together with certain data in the case, which the Congregations will want to have. Moreover, equity and respect recommend that a subject notify his superior that he is referring the decree of removal to the judgment of the Holy See.

It should duly be noted here that if a cleric is removed or rather deprived of his office by way of a vindictive penalty for a crime he has committed, then it seems that the ordinary must be notified of the recourse made to the Holy See. For the recourse in this instance has, as a rule, a suspensive effect.[13] As McClunn holds, it seems that when the law allows a recourse with suspensive effect, it presupposes that the ordinary or the superior will be notified that his decree or penalty has been deprived of the efficacy it previously had.[14] Otherwise he would learn of this important effect only after some time, namely, when he is requested by the Holy See to transmit pertinent acts and data on the case in question.

In the event that the ordinary is notified of the intended recourse, or when he is requested by the Sacred Congregation to forward the pertinent acts and data, what acts and data are to be sent to the Holy See by the ordinary? In general, all documents, or at least authentic copies of the same, which pertain to the decree of removal and to the alleged injustice or detriment to rights or interests make up the acts and data (*acta negotii*) in the case. Included among these documents should be an authentic copy of the decree of removal. Likewise the ordinary should state the circumstances of and the reasons for decreeing the removal. This will forestall any possible future delay at least on this score. The ordinary or the superior must also forward whatever proof is necessary to show the justice of his action.[15]

---

[13] Canon 2287; McClunn, *op. cit.*, pp. 60-61.

[14] *Administrative Recourse*, pp. 39-41.

[15] Cf. McClunn, *op. cit.*, pp. 43-50.

Finally, it must be noted that no time limit is set by the law within which the recourse mentioned in canon 192, § 3, must be made to the Holy See, such as is demanded for the suspensive effect of the recourse undertaken by a pastor against the definitive decree of removal in the administrative process of canon 2146.[16] The recourse against a decree of simple removal may be made any time. There is no need for any set time-limit. Since this recourse has only a non-suspensive effect, the ordinary knows that his decree has taken effect, and the subject who is removed knows that he is free at any time to take his recourse to the Holy See.

SECTION III. THE SUPERIOR TO WHOM THE RECOURSE IS TO BE MADE

According to the present law the Sacred Congregations have an exclusive right to receive recourses against the decrees issued by ordinaries.[17]

Most recourses in the matter of simple removal from office are to be sent to the Sacred Congregation of the Council. This is the Congregation which is competent to receive the recourses of the secular clerics from all legislative, executive and administrative decrees of their local ordinaries.[18]

Since, however, the Sacred Congregation of Religious has exclusive authority over the government and discipline of religious, it is this Congregation which is competent to receive all recourses which affect the rights or interests of any religious as such.[19] It is important to stress the fact that this Congregation is competent in matters which affect the religious as such. So when the ques-

---

[16] S.C.C., *Romana et aliarum,* 14 ian. 1924: "Tempus utile ad recursum interponendum a definitivo decreto remotionis, ad effectum § 3 can. 2146 Codicis, esse decemdium ab intimatione eiusdem decreti, supputandum ad normam can. 34, § 3, 3°, et can. 35; certiore facto Ordinario loci ab ipso recurrente de legitime interposito recursu ad Apostolicam Sedem."—*AAS,* XVI (1924), 165; Bouscaren, *The Canon Law Digest,* I, 837.

[17] "Contra Ordinariorum decreta non datur appellatio seu recursus ad Sacram Rotam; sed de eiusmodi recursibus exclusive cognoscunt Sacrae Congregationes."—Canon 1601.

[18] Canon 250.

[19] Canon 251, § 1.

tion of removal from office directly affects a person as a religious, he makes his recourse to the Sacred Congregation of Religious. But, when the removal affects him as a religious only indirectly, he must make his recourse to the Sacred Congregation of the Council.[20] Thus, for example, a religious pastor makes his recourse to the Sacred Congregation of the Council against a decree of removal issued by the local ordinary, for in this matter he makes the recourse not as a religious but as a pastor.[21] Moreover, if the religious makes recourse against a decree of removal effected by a vicar or prefect apostolic, he sends it to the Sacred Congregation for the Propagation of the Faith. Again, if the religious belongs to an Oriental Rite, he makes his recourse to the Sacred Congregation for the Oriental Church.[22] For in missionary countries and in regions where the hierarchy is established but still in its initial stage, the competent authority for receiving recourses is the Sacred Congregation for the Propagation of the Faith.[23] But matters which affect the persons or the discipline of the Oriental Churches fall under the jurisdiction of the Sacred Congregation for the Oriental Church.[24]

In the possible event of doubt regarding which Congregation is competent in a given case, the recourse may be sent to the Secretariate of State, which in turn will forward it to the proper authority.

SECTION IV. THE EFFECT OF THE RECOURSE

As already mentioned, the recourse available to a cleric through the ruling of canon 192, § 3, has only a non-suspensive effect (*in devolutivo tantum*). In contrast to a recourse which has a suspensive effect, and which therefore denotes that the execution of a decree is prohibited until the entire case is reviewed, the recourse with a non-suspensive effect denotes that the issue is brought be-

---

[20] Cf. McClunn, *Administrative Recourse,* p. 79.
[21] Cf. canons 454, § 5; 631, § 1.
[22] Canon 257.
[23] Canon 252, §§ 3, 5.
[24] Canon 257, § 1.

fore a superior, but, while he is judging on the merits of the case, the previous decree of the ordinary remains operative in its effect.[25]

While the recourse is pending, this circumstance in no way interferes with the jurisdiction of the ordinary, nor does it retard the execution of his decree of removal. Thus the ordinary or the superior is free to confer the office on another.[26] However, the authority from whom the recourse is made must do nothing to interfere with the redress that is being sought with the Holy See.

---

[25] Cf. canon 1889, § 1; Wernz-Vidal, *Ius Canonicum,* III, n. 607; Vermeersch-Creusen, *Epitome,* III, n. 240; McClunn, *Administrative Recourse,* p. 88.

[26] Berutti, *Institutiones Iuris Canonici,* II, 302.

CONCLUSIONS

1. The historical basis for simple removal from office is to be found in the sharp contrast between those offices which go back to antiquity and those which the Church created in the later Middle Ages in order to meet the demands of administrative needs (pp. 3, 9).

2. The first clear mention of such removal appears in the remarks of the glossator upon a Decretal of Pope Clement V (1305-1314), where it is noted that the vicar general was removable *ad nutum* (pp. 9-10).

3. The lack of subjective permanency in office which gave rise to the type of removal called a simple removal or also a removal made *ad nutum* had its basis in the essential difference between manual and non-manual benefices (pp. 10-11).

4. Among the historical predecessors of the office of vicar forane, there are some indications that the rural deans, inasfar as they were at times temporary vicars, could be removed from office by a simple renewal for a reasonable cause (pp. 12-14).

5. Canon 192, § 3, applies directly to ecclesiastical offices in the strict sense (pp. 35, 55-56). But by analogy, in virtue of canon 20, the same principles are to be applied with reference to offices in the wide sense (pp. 56, 80-81).

6. With the exception of parochial vicars, the vicar general is competent to decree the simple removal from office (pp. 47-49), although in practice he should not use this power without consulting the bishop. The same conclusion applies to the vicar delegate of a vicar or a prefect apostolic.

7. Aside from the express exceptions contained in the law, the vicar capitular or the administrator of a vacant see is also competent with regard to the simple removal from office (p. 50).

8. Local superiors of religious institutes who are, by reason of the constitutions of their institute, competent to remove incumbents from office are bound also to follow the norms of canon 192, § 3 (p. 54).

9. The requirements of canon 192, § 3, must be observed in the removal of incumbents who are designated as removable *ad nutum*. Their removal is not therefore a purely arbitrary affair (p. 56).

10. Inasfar as, in a given case, the canon penitentiary is removable, he can be removed from his office by a simple removal. But it is proper, though not necessary, that the bishop consult the cathedral chapter in this matter (pp. 61-62).

11. Of the pastors mentioned in canon 454, the only ones who are subject to simple removal are those who belong to some religious institute. The same rule, it seems, would apply to those pastors who are members of societies which after the fashion of religious live the common life (p. 66).

12. By analogy, secular priest chaplains of pious associations of the faithful erected by religious in their own churches are removable *ad nutum* (p. 75).

13. If a chaplaincy has been erected into a manual benefice, the incumbent may be removed according to the norms of canon 192, § 3 (pp. 77-78).

14. The judge in an ecclesiastical trial can by simple removal remove a notary whom he has appointed for a particular case (pp. 82-83).

15. The requirements in canon 192, § 3, of the presence of a just cause and of the observance of natural equity do not touch the factor of validity for the act of removal, but simply the element of lawfulness (p. 94).

16. Whenever the ordinary makes use of the power given him in canon 192, § 3, he has the moral obligation to see to it that the equitable rights of the cleric who is to be removed from office do not suffer any undeserved infringement. This obligation is founded not on charity nor on mercy but rather on the virtue of justice as its root, without however implying the necessity of restitution. The equity involved which is founded on the possession of an office demands as a minimum that there be a recompense for the loss of the office, if that loss is beyond what is to be expected in line with the spirit of sacrifice normally demanded by the priesthood (p. 104 ff.).

BIBLIOGRAPHY

Sources

Acta Apostolicae Sedis, Commentarium Officiale, Romae, 1909-

Acta et Decreta, Concilii Plenarii Baltimorensis Tertii, A. D. MDCCCLXXXIV, Baltimorae: Typis Joannis Murphy et Sociorum, 1886.

Acta Sanctae Sedis, 41 vols., Romae, 1865-1908.

Bullarum Diplomatum et Privilegiorum Sanctorum Romanorum Pontificum Taurinensis Editio, 24 vols. et Appendix, Augustae Taurinorum, 1857-1872.

Codex Iuris Canonici Pii X Pontificis Maximi iussu digestus Benedicti Papae XV auctoritate promulgatus praefatione fontium annotatione et indice analytico-alphabetico ab Emo Card. Gasparri ductus, Romae: Typis Polyglottis Vaticanis, 1917 (special ed., Westminster, Maryland: The Newman Book Shop, 1944).

Codicis Iuris Canonici Fontes cura Emi Card. Gasparri editi, 9 vols., Romae (postea Civitate Vaticana): Typis Polyglottis Vaticanis, 1923-1939 (Vols. VII-IX ed. cura et studio Emi Iustiniani Card. Serédi).

Concilii Plenarii Baltimorensis II, in Ecclesia Metropolitana Baltimorensi, a die VII ad diem XXI Octobris, A.D. MDCCCLXVI, Habiti, et a Sede Apostolica Recogniti, Acta et Decreta, Baltimorae: John Murphy, 1868.

Constitutiones Fratrum Sacri Ordinis Praedicatorum Inchoatae in Capitulo Generali Provincialium Romae celebrato a. 1924, Romae: Ex Typographia R. Garroni, 1925.

Corpus Iuris Canonici, ed. Lipsiensis 2. post Aemilii Ludovici Richteri curas . . . instruxit Aemilius Friedberg, Lipsiae: Ex Officina Bernhardi Tauchnitz, 1879-1881; ed. anastatice repetita, Lipsiae: Tauchnitz, 1928.

Jaffé, Philippus, *Regesta Pontificum Romanorum ab condita Ecclesia ad annum post Christum natum MCXCVIII,* ed. 2. correctam et auctam auspiciis Gulielmi Wattenbach curaverunt S. Loewenfeld, F. Kaltenbrunner, P. Ewald, 2 vols., Lipsiae, 1885-1888.

Mansi, Joannes, *Sacrorum Conciliorum Nova et Amplissima Collectio,* 53 vols. in 60, Parisiis-Arnhem-Leipzig, 1901-1927.

Potthast, Augustus, *Regesta Pontificum Romanorum inde ab anno post Christum natum MCXCVIII ad annum MCCCIV,* 2 vols., Berolini, 1874-1875.

Schroeder, H., *Canons and Decrees of the Council of Trent,* St. Louis: B. Herder Book Co., 1941.

The Rule and General Constitutions of the Friars Minor, Paterson, New Jersey: St. Anthony Guild Press, 1936.

REFERENCE WORKS

Augustine, C., *A Commentary on the New Code of Canon Law,* 8 vols., St. Louis: Herder & Co., 1925-1938, Vol. II, 6. ed., 1936; Vol. VII, 3. ed., 1930.

Ayrinhac, H. A., *Constitution of the Church in the New Code of Canon Law,* New York: Benziger & Co., 1925.

———, *General Legislation in the New Code of Canon Law,* New York: Benziger & Co., 1923.

Bastnagel, C., *The Appointment of Parochial Adjutants and Assistants,* The Catholic University of America Canon Law Studies, n. 58, Washington, D. C.: The Catholic University of America, 1930.

Berutti, C., *Institutiones Iuris Canonici,* 6 vols., Vol. II, Pars I, Taurini: Marietti, 1943.

Beste, Udalricus, *Introductio in Codicem,* 2. ed., Collegeville, Minn.: St. John's Abbey Press, 1944.

Blat, Albertus, *Commentarium Textus Codicis Iuris Canonici,* 5 vols. in 7, Romae: Ex Typographia Pontificia in Instituto Pii X, 1921-1927, Vol. II, 2. ed., 1921.

Bouscaren, T., *The Canon Law Digest,* 2 vols., Milwaukee: Bruce, 1934-1943.

Bouscaren, T.,-Ellis, A., *Canon Law, A Text and Commentary,* Milwaukee: Bruce, 1946.

Cappello, Felix, *Summa Iuris Canonici,* 3 vols., Romae: Apud Aedes Universitatis Gregorianae, Vol. I, 4. ed., 1925; Vol. II, 4. ed., 1945; Vol. III, 2. ed., 1940.

Chelodi, Ioannes, *Ius de Personis,* 2. ed., Tridenti: Libr. Edit. Tridentum, 1927.

Claeys-Bouuaert, F., *De Canonica Cleri Saecularis Obedientia,* Lovanii, 1904.

Claeys-Bouuaert, F.-Simenon, G., *Manuale Juris Canonici ad usum Seminariorum,* 3 vols., Vol. I, 3. ed., Gandae et Leodii: Seminarium Gandavense et Leodiense, 1930.

Clancy, P., *The Local Religious Superior,* The Catholic University of America Canon Law Studies, n. 175, Washington, D. C.: The Catholic University of America Press, 1943.

Clarke, T., *Parish Societies,* The Catholic University of America Canon Law Studies, n. 176, Washington, D. C.: The Catholic University of America Press, 1943.

Cocchi, Guidus, *Commentarium in Codicem Iuris Canonici,* 8 vols. in 5, Vol. II, 4. ed., Taurinorum Augustae: Marietti, 1937.

Connolly, J. *Synodal Examiners and Parish Priest Consultors,* The Catholic University of America Canon Law Studies, n. 177, Washington, D. C.: The Catholic University of America Press, 1943.

Connor, Maurice, *The Administrative Removal of Pastors,* The Catholic University of America Canon Law Studies, n. 104, Washington, D. C.: The Catholic University of America, 1937.

Coronata, Matthaeus Conte a, *Institutiones Iuris Canonici,* 5 vols., Vol. I, 2. ed., 1939; Vol. III, ed. altera, 1941, Taurini: Marietti.

Cox, J., *The Administration of Seminaries,* The Catholic University of America Canon Law Studies, n. 67, Washington, D. C.: The Catholic University of America, 1931.

De Meester, A., *Juris Canonici et Juris Canonico-Civilis Compendium,* ed. nova, 3 vols. in 4, Brugis: Desclée, 1921-1928.

Drumm, W., *Hospital Chaplains,* The Catholic University of America Canon Law Studies, n. 178, Washington, D. C.: The Catholic University of America Press, 1943.

Dugan, H., *The Judiciary Department of the Diocesan Curia,* The Catholic University of America Canon Law Studies, n. 26, Washington, D. C.: The Catholic University of America, 1925.

Fagnanus, Prosper, *Commentaria in Quinque Libros Decretalium,* 5 vols. in 3, Venetiis, 1709.

Ferraris, Lucius, *Prompta Bibliotheca, Canonica, Iuridica, Moralis, Theologica necnon Ascetica, Polemica, Rubricistica, Historica,* 9 vols., Romae, 1885-1899.

Galvin, W. A., *The Administrative Transfer of Pastors,* The Catholic University of America Canon Law Studies, n. 232, Washington, D. C.: The Catholic University of America Press, 1946.

Hostiensis, Cardinalis (Henricus de Segusio), *Commentaria in Quinque Decretalium Libros,* 5 vols. in 3, Venetiis, 1581.

Klekotka, P., *Diocesan Consultors,* The Catholic University of America Canon Law Studies, n. 8, Washington, D. C.: The Catholic University of America, 1920.

Lynch, G., *Coadjutors and Auxiliaries of Bishops,* The Catholic University of America Canon Law Studies, n. 238, Washington, D. C.: The Catholic University of America Press, 1947.

Manning, J., *The Free Conferral of Offices,* The Catholic University of America Canon Law Studies, n. 219, Washington, D. C.: The Catholic University of America Press, 1945.

Maroto, Philippus, *Institutiones Iuris Canonici,* 2 vols., Vol. I, 3. ed., Romae: Apud Commentarium pro Religiosis, 1921.

McBride, J., *Incardination and Excardination of Seculars,* The Catholic University of America Canon Law Studies, n. 145, Washington, D. C.: The Catholic University of America Press, 1941.

McClunn, J., *Administrative Recourse,* The Catholic University of America Canon Law Studies, n. 240, Washington, D. C.: The Catholic University of America Press, 1946.

McDevitt, G., *The Renunciation of an Ecclesiastical Office,* The Catholic University of America Canon Law Studies, n. 218, Washington, D. C.: The Catholic University of America Press, 1946.

Meier, C., *Penal Administrative Procedure Against Negligent Pastors,* The Catholic University of America Canon Law Studies, n. 140, Washington, D. C.: The Catholic University of America Press, 1941.

Ojetti, B., *Commentarium in Codicem Iuris Canonici,* 4 vols., Romae: Apud Aedes Universitatis Gregorianae, 1927-1931.

Pistocchi, Marius, *De Re Beneficiali iuxta Canones Codicis Iuris Canonici,* Taurini: Marietti, 1928.

Prince, J., *The Diocesan Chancellor,* The Catholic University of America Canon Law Studies, n. 167, Washington, D. C.: The Catholic University of America Press, 1942.

Prümmer, D., *Manuale Iuris Canonici in Usum Scholarum,* 3. ed., Friburgi Brisgoviae, 1922.

Reiffenstuel, Anacletus, *Jus Canonicum Universum,* 5 vols. in 6, Romae, 1831-1835.

Roberti, Franciscus, *De Processibus,* 2 vols., Vol. I, 2. ed., Romae: Apud Custodiam Librariam Pontificii Instituti Utriusque Iuris, 1941.

Schaefer, T., *De Religiosis ad Normam Codicis Iuris Canonici,* 3. ed., Romae: Typis Polyglottis Vaticanis, 1940.

Schmalzgrueber, F., *Jus Ecclesiasticum Universum,* 5 vols. in 12, Romae: 1843-1845.

Sipos, Stephanus, *Enchiridion Iuris Canonici ad usum scholarum et privatorum,* Pécs: ex Typographia "Haladás R.T.," 1926.

Thomassinus, L., *Vetus et Nova Ecclesiae Disciplina circa Beneficia et Beneficiarios,* 10 vols., Magontiaci, 1787.

Toso, A., *Ad Codicem Iuris Canonici . . . Commentaria Minora,* 5 vols., Romae: Marietti, 1920-1927.

Vermeersch, A.-Creusen, J., *Epitome Iuris Canonici,* 3 vols., Vol. I, 6. ed., Mechliniae et Romae: Dessain, 1937.

Wernz, F. X., *Ius Decretalium,* 2. ed., 6 vols., Romae et Prati, 1906-1913. Vol. II, 3. ed., Prati, 1915.

Wernz, F. X.-Vidal, P., *Ius Canonicum,* 7 vols. in 8, Vol. II, 2. ed., Romae: Apud Aedes Universitatis Gregorianae, 1928.

Zaplotnik, Ioannes L., *De Vicariis Foraneis,* The Catholic University of America Canon Law Studies, n. 47, Washington, D. C.: The Catholic University of America, 1927.

Articles

D'Angelo, S., "De Aequitate in Codice Iuris Canonici"—*Apollinaris,* I (1928), 363-383.

Roelker, E., "The Meaning of 'Aequitas,' 'Aequus,' and 'Aeque' in the Code of Canon Law"—*The Jurist,* VI (1946), 239-274.

Sipos, S., "Ad officium sacrum an requiratur potestas ordinaria?"—*Jus Pontificium,* XVI (1936), 67-68.

Periodicals

Apollinaris, Romae: Apud Aedes Facultatis Iuridicae, 1928-

Jurist, The, Washington, D. C., 1941-

Jus Pontificium, Romae, 1921-1940.

ABBREVIATIONS

AAS—*Acta Apostolicae Sedis.*
Acta et Decreta—*Concilii Plenarii Baltimorensis Secundi Acta et Decreta.*
ASS—*Acta Sanctae Sedis.*
Fontes—*Codicis Iuris Canonici Fontes cura . . . Gasparri editi.*
Jaffé—*Regesta Pontificum Romanorum etc.*
Mansi—*Sacrorum Conciliorum Nova et Amplissima Collectio.*
Potthast—*Regesta Pontificum Romanorum etc.*
S.C.C.—Sacra Congregatio Concilii.
S.C. de Prop. Fide—Sacra Congregatio de Propaganda Fide.
S.C. Ep. et Reg.—Sacra Congregatio Episcoporum et Regularium.
S.R.R.—Sacra Romana Rota.

BIOGRAPHICAL NOTE

Chester Joseph Thompson was born on August 25, 1918, in San Francisco, California. He attended Grant School in that city. In 1932 he entered St. Joseph's College, Mountain View, California, the preparatory seminary for the Archdiocese of San Francisco. In 1938 he entered St. Patrick's Seminary, Menlo Park, California, and with the completion of his philosophy course received the degree of Bachelor of Arts. He was ordained to the Holy Priesthood at St. Mary's Cathedral, San Francisco, on December 18, 1943. After two years of parochial work in Oakland, California, he was assigned to the Catholic University of America to pursue a course of studies in the School of Canon Law. He received the Baccalaureate Degree in Canon Law in June, 1946, and the Licentiate Degree in Canon Law in June, 1947.

ALPHABETICAL INDEX

CANON LAW STUDIES*

1. FRERIKS, REV. CELESTINE A., C.PP.S., J.C.D., Religious Congregations in Their External Relations, 121 pp. 1916.
2. GALLIHER, REV. DANIEL M., O.P., J.C.D., Canonical Elections, 117 pp., 1917.
3. BORKOWSKI, REV. AURELIUS L., O.F.M., J.C.D., De Confraternibus Ecclesiasticis, 136 pp., 1918.
4. CASTILLO, REV. CAYO, J.C.D., Disertacion Historico-Canonica sobre la Potestad del Cabildo en Sede Vacante o Impedida del Vicario Capitular, 99 pp., 1919 (1918).
5. KUBELBECK, REV. WILLIAM J., S.T.B., J.C.D., The Sacred Penitentiaria and Its Relation to Faculties of Ordinaries and Priests, 129 pp., 1918.
6. PETROVITS, REV. JOSEPH, J.C., S.T.D., J.C.D., The New Church Law on Matrimony, X-461 pp., 1919.
7. HICKEY, REV. JOHN J., S.T.B., J.C.D., Irregularities and Simple Impediments in the New Code of Canon Law, 100 pp., 1920.
8. KLEKOTKA, REV. PETER J., S.T.B., J.C.D., Diocesan Consultors, 179 pp., 1920.
9. WANENMACHER, REV. FRANCIS, J.C.D., The Evidence in Ecclesiastical Procedure Affecting the Marriage Bond, 1920 (Printed 1935).
10. GOLDEN, REV. HENRY FRANCIS, J.C.D., Parochial Benefices in the New Code, IV-119 pp., 1921 (Printed 1925).
11. KOUDELKA, REV. CHARLES J., J.C.D., Pastors, Their Rights and Duties According to the New Code of Canon Law, 211 pp., 1921.
12. MELO, REV. ANTONIUS, O.F.M., J.C.D., De Exemptione Regularium, X-188 pp., 1921
13. SCHAAF, REV. VALENTINE THEODORE, O.F.M., S.T.B., J.C.D., The Cloister, X-180 pp., 1921.
14. BURKE, REV. THOMAS JOSEPH, S.T.D., J.C.D., Competence in Ecclesiastical Tribunals, IV-117 pp., 1922.
15. LEECH, REV. GEORGE LEO, J.C.D., A Comparative Study of the Constitution "Apostolicae Sedis" and the "Codex Juris Canonici," 179 pp., 1922.
16. MOTRY, REV. HUBERT LOUIS, S.T.D., J.C.D., Diocesan Faculties According to the Code of Canon Law, II-167 pp., 1922.
17. MURPHY, REV. GEORGE LAWRENCE, J.C.D., Delinquencies and Penalties in the Administration and the Reception of the Sacraments, IV-121 pp., 1923.

*All published numbers are available from the Catholic University of America Press, 620 Michigan Avenue, N.E., Washington 17, D. C., except the following: Nos. 1-114 inclusive, 115, 118, 120, 122, 123, 136, 153, 162, 182 and 198. But the following numbers, now reissued, are obtainable from *The Jurist*, The Catholic University of America, Washington 17, D. C., namely: Nos. 5, 7, 11, 17, 18, 19, 26, 28, 30, 31, 34, 42, 44, 51, 52 and 61.

18. O'Reilly, Rev. John Anthony, S.T.B., J.C.D., Ecclesiastical Sepulture in the New Code of Canon Law, II-129 pp., 1923.
19. Michalicka, Rev. Wenceslas Cyrill, O.S.B., J.C.D., Judicial Procedure in Dismissal of Clerical Exempt Religious, 107 pp., 1923.
20. Dargin, Rev. Edward Vincent, S.T.B., J.C.D., Reserved Cases According to the Code of Canon Law, IV-103 pp., 1924.
21. Godfrey, Rev. John A., S.T.B., J.C.D., The Right of Patronage According to the Code of Canon Law, 153 pp., 1924.
22. Hagedorn, Rev. Francis Edward, J.C.D., General Legislation on Indulgences, II-154 pp., 1924.
23. King, Rev. James Ignatius, J.C.D., The Administration of the Sacraments to Dying Non-Catholics, V-141 pp., 1924.
24. Winslow, Rev. Francis Joseph, O.F.M., J.C.D., Vicars and Prefects Apostolic, IV-149 pp., 1924.
25. Correa, Rev. Jose Servelion, S.T.L., J.C.D., La Potestad Legislativa de la Iglesia Catolica, IV-127 pp., 1925.
26. Dugan, Rev. Henry Francis, A.M., J.C.D., The Judiciary Department of the Diocesan Curia, 87 pp., 1925.
27. Keller, Rev. Charles Frederick, S.T.B., J.C.D., Mass Stipends, 167 pp., 1925.
28. Paschang, Rev. John Linus, J.C.D., The Sacramentals According to the Code of Canon Law, 129 pp., 1925.
29. Piontek, Rev. Cyrillus, O.F.M., S.T.B., J.C.D., De Indulto Exclaustrationis necnon Saecularizationis, XIII-289 pp., 1925.
30. Kearney, Rev. Richard Joseph, S.T.B., J.C.D., Sponsors at Baptism According to the Code of Canon Law, IV-127 pp., 1925.
31. Bartlett, Rev. Chester Joseph, A.M., LL.B., J.C.D., The Tenure of Parochial Property in the United States of America, V-108 pp., 1926.
32. Kilker, Rev. Adrian Jerome, J.C.D., Extreme Unction, V-425 pp., 1926.
33. McCormick, Rev. Robert Emmett, J.C.D., Confessors of Religious, VIII-266 pp., 1926.
34. Miller, Rev. Newton Thomas, J.C.D., Founded Masses According to the Code of Canon Law, VII-93 pp., 1926.
35. Roelker, Rev. Edward G., S.T.D., J.C.D., Principles of Privilege According to the Code of Canon Law, XI-166 pp., 1926.
36. Bakalarczyk, Rev. Richardus, M.I.C., J.U.D., De Novitiatu, VIII-208 pp., 1927.
37. Pizzuti, Rev. Lawrence, O.F.M., J.U.L., De Parochis Religiosis, 1927. (Not Printed.)
38. Bliley, Rev. Nicholas Martin, O.S.B., J.C.D., Altars According to the Code of Canon Law, XIX-132 pp., 1927.
39. Brown, Mr. Brendan Francis, A.B., LL.M., J.U.D., The Canonical Juristic Personality with Special Reference to its Status in the United States of America, V-212 pp., 1927.

40. CAVANAUGH, REV. WILLIAM THOMAS, C.P., J.U.D., The Reservation of the Blessed Sacrament, VIII-101 pp., 1927.
41. DOHENY, REV. WILLIAM J., C.S.C., A.B., J.C.D., Church Property: Modes of Acquisition, X-118 pp., 1927.
42. FELDHAUS, REV. ALOYSIUS H., C.PP.S., J.C.D., Oratories, IV-141 pp., 1927.
43. KELLY, REV. JAMES PATRICK, A.B., J.C.D., The Jurisdiction of the Simple Confessor, X-208 pp., 1927.
44. NEUBERGER, REV. NICHOLAS J., J.C.D., Canon 6 or the Relation of the Codex Iuris Canonici to the Preceding Legislation, V-95 pp., 1927.
45. O'KEEFE, REV. GERALD MICHAEL, J.C.D., Matrimonial Dispensations, Powers of Bishops, Priests, and Confessors, VIII-232 pp., 1927.
46. QUIGLEY, REV. JOSEPH A. M., A.B., J.C.D., Condemned Societies, 139 pp., 1927.
47. ZAPLOTNIK, REV. JOHANNES LEO, J.C.D., De Vicariis Foraneis, X-142 pp., 1927.
48. DUSKIE, REV. JOHN ALOYSIUS, A.B., J.C.D., The Canonical Status of the Orientals in the United States, VIII-196 pp., 1928.
49. HYLAND, REV. FRANCIS EDWARD, J.C.D., Excommunication, Its Nature, Historical Development and Effects, VIII-181 pp., 1928.
50. REIMANN, REV. GERALD JOSEPH, O.M.C., J.C.D., The Third Order Secular of Saint Francis, 201 pp., 1928.
51. SCHENK, REV. FRANCIS J., J.C.D., The Matrimonial Impediments of Mixed Religion and Disparity of Cult, XVI-318 pp., 1929.
52. COADY, REV. JOHN JOSEPH, S.T.D., J.U.D., A.M., The Appointment of Pastors, VIII-150 pp., 1929.
53. KAY, REV. THOMAS HENRY, J.C.D., Competence in Matrimonial Procedure, VIII-164 pp., 1929.
54. TURNER, REV. SIDNEY JOSEPH, C.P., J.U.D., The Vow of Poverty, XLIX-217 pp., 1929.
55. KEARNEY, REV. RAYMOND A., A.B., S.T.D., J.C.D., The Principles of Delegation, VII-149 pp., 1929.
56. CONRAN, REV. EDWARD JAMES, A.B., J.C.D., The Interdict, V-163 pp., 1930.
57. O'NEILL, REV. WILLIAM H., J.C.D., Papal Rescripts of Favor, VII-218 pp., 1930.
58. BASTNAGEL, REV. CLEMENT VINCENT, J.U.D., The Appointment of Parochial Adjutants and Assistants, XV-257 pp., 1930.
59. FERRY, REV. WILLIAM A., A.B., J.C.D., Stole Fees, V-136 pp., 1930.
60. COSTELLO, REV. JOHN MICHAEL, A.B., J.C.D., Domicile and Quasi-Domicile, VII-201 pp., 1930.
61. KREMER, REV. MICHAEL NICHOLAS, A.B., S.T.B., J.C.D., Church Support in the United States, VI-136 pp., 1930.
62. ANGULO, REV. LUIS, C.M., J.C.D., Legislation de la Iglesia sobre la intencion en la application de la Santa Misa, VII-104 pp., 1931.

63. FREY, REV. WOLFGANG NORBERT, O.S.B., A.B., J.C.D., The Act of Religious Profession, VIII-174 pp., 1931.
64. ROBERTS, REV. JAMES BRENDAN, A.B., J.C.D., The Banns of Marriage, XIV-140 pp., 1931.
65. RYDER, REV. RAYMOND ALOYSIUS, A.B., J.C.D., Simony, IX-151 pp., 1931.
66. CAMPAGNA, REV. ANGELO, PH.D., J.U.D., Il Vicario Generale del Vescovo, VII-205, pp., 1931.
67. COX, REV. JOSEPH GODFREY, A.B., J.C.D., The Administration of Seminaries, VI-124 pp., 1931.
68. GREGORY, REV. DONALD J., J.U.D., The Pauline Privilege, XV-165 pp., 1931.
69. DONOHUE, REV. JOHN F., J.C.D., The Impediment of Crime, VII-110 pp., 1931.
70. DOOLEY, REV. EUGENE A., O.M.I., J.C.D., Church Law on Sacred Relics, IX-143 pp., 1931.
71. ORTH, REV. CLEMENT RAYMOND, O.M.C., J.C.D., The Approbation of Religious Institutes, 171 pp., 1931.
72. PERNICONE, REV. JOSEPH M., A.B., J.C.D., The Ecclesiastical Prohibition of Books, XII-267 pp., 1932.
73. CLINTON, REV. CONNELL, A.B., J.C.D., The Paschal Precept, IX-108 pp., 1932.
74. DONNELLY, REV. FRANCIS B., A.M., S.T.L., J.C.D., The Diocesan Synod, VIII-125 pp., 1932.
75. TORRENTE, REV. CAMILO, C.M.F., J.C.D., Las Procesiones Sagradas, V-145 pp., 1932.
76. MURPHY, REV. EDWIN J., C.PP.S., J.C.D., Suspension Ex Informata Conscientia, XI-122 pp., 1932.
77. MACKENZIE, REV. ERIC F., A.M., S.T.L., J.C.D., The Delict of Heresy in its Commission, Penalization, Absolution, VII-124 pp., 1932.
78. LYONS, REV. AVITUS E., S.T.B., J.C.D., The Collegiate Tribunal of First Instance, XI-147 pp., 1932.
79. CONNOLLY, REV. THOMAS A., J.C.D., Appeals, XI-195 pp., 1932.
80. SANGMEISTER, REV. JOSEPH V., A.B., J.C.D., Force and Fear as Precluding Matrimonial Consent, V-211 pp., 1932.
81. JAEGER, REV. LEO A., A.B., J.C.D., The Administration of Vacant and Quasi-Vacant Episcopal Sees in the United States, IX-229 pp., 1932.
82. RIMLINGER, REV. HERBERT T., J.C.D., Error Invalidating Matrimonial Consent, VII-79 pp., 1932.
83. BARRETT, REV. JOHN D. M., S.S., J.C.D., A Comparative Study of the Councils of Baltimore and the Code of Canon Law, IX-223 pp., 1932.
84. CARBERRY, REV. JOHN J., PH.D., S.T.D., J.C.D., The Juridical Form of Marriage, X-177 pp., 1934.
85. DOLAN, REV. JOHN L., A.B., J.C.D., The Defensor Vinculi, XII-157 pp., 1934.

86. HANNAN, REV. JEROME D., A.M., S.T.D., LL.B., J.C.D., The Canon Law of Wills, IX-517 pp., 1934.
87. LEMIEUX, REV. DELISE A., A.M., J.C.D., The Sentence in Ecclesiastical Procedure, IX-131 pp., 1934.
88. O'ROURKE, REV. JAMES J., A.B., J.C.D., Parish Registers, VII-109 pp., 1934.
89. TIMLIN, REV. BARTHOLOMEW, O.F.M., A.M., J.C.D., Conditional Matrimonial Consent, X-381 pp., 1934.
90. WAHL, REV. FRANCIS X., A.B., J.C.D., The Matrimonial Impediments of Consanguinity and Affinity, VI-125 pp., 1934.
91. WHITE, REV. ROBERT J., A.B., LL.B., S.T.B., J.C.D., Canonical Ante-Nuptial Promises and the Civil Law, VI-152 pp., 1934.
92. HERRERA, REV. ANTONIO PARRA, O.C.D., J.C.D., Legislacion Ecclesiastica sobra el Ayuno y la Abstinencia, XI-191 pp., 1935.
93. KENNEDY, REV. EDWIN J., J.C.D., The Special Matrimonial Process in Cases of Evident Nullity, X-165 pp., 1935.
94. MANNING, REV. JOHN J., A.B., J.C.D., Presumption of Law in Matrimonial Procedure, XI-111 pp., 1935.
95. MOEDER, REV. JOHN M., J.C.D., The Proper Bishop for Ordination and Dismissorial Letters, VII-135 pp., 1935.
96. O'MARA, REV. WILLIAM A., A.B., J.C.D., Canonical Causes for Matrimonial Dispensations, IX-155 pp., 1935.
97. REILLY, REV. PETER, J.C.D., Residence of Pastors, IX-81 pp., 1935.
98. SMITH, REV. MARINER T., O.P., S.T.Lr., J.C.D., The Penal Law for Religious, VIII-169 pp., 1935.
99. WHALEN, REV. DONALD W., A.M., J.C.D., The Value of Testimonial Evidence in Matrimonial Procedure, XIII-297 pp., 1935.
100. CLEARY, REV. JOSEPH F., J.C.D., Canonical Limitations on the Alienation of Church Property, VIII-141 pp., 1936.
101. GLYNN, REV. JOHN C., J.C.D., The Promoter of Justice, XX-337 pp., 1936.
102. BRENNAN, REV. JAMES H., S.S., M.A., S.T.B., J.C.D., The Simple Convalidation of Marriage, VI-135 pp., 1937.
103. BRUNINI, REV. JOSEPH BERNARD, J.C.D., The Clerical Obligations of Canons 139 and 142, X-121 pp., 1937.
104. CONNOR, REV. MAURICE, A.B., J.C.D., The Administrative Removal of Pastors, VIII-159 pp., 1937.
105. GUILFOYLE, REV. MERLIN JOSEPH, J.C.D., Custom, XI-144 pp., 1937.
106. HUGHES, REV. JAMES AUSTIN, A.B., A.M., J.C.D., Witnesses in Criminal Trials of Clerics, IX-140 pp., 1937.
107. JANSEN, REV. RAYMOND J., A.B., S.T.L., J.C.D., Canonical Provisions for Catechetical Instruction, VII-153 pp., 1937.
108. KEALY, REV. JOHN JAMES, A.B., J.C.D., The Introductory Libellus in Church Court Procedure, XI-121 pp., 1937.

109. McManus, Rev. James Edward, C.SS.R., J.C.D., The Administration of Temporal Goods in Religious Institutes, XVI-196 pp., 1937.
110. Moriarty, Rev. Eugene James, J.C.D., Oaths in Ecclesiastical Courts, X-115 pp., 1937.
111. Rainer, Reg. Eligius George, C.SS.R., J.C.D., Suspension of Clerics, XVII-249 pp., 1937.
112. Reilly, Rev. Thomas F., C.SS.R., J.C.D., Visitation of Religious, VI-195 pp., 1938.
113. Moriarty, Rev. Francis E., C.SS.R., J.C.D., The Extraordinary Absolution from Censures, XV-334 pp., 1938.
114. Connolly, Rev. Nicholas P., J.C.D., The Canonical Erection of Parishes, X-132 pp., 1938.
115. Donovan, Rev. James Joseph, J.C.D., The Pastor's Obligation in Prenuptial Investigation, XII-322 pp., 1938.
116. Harrigan, Rev. Robert J., M.A., S.T.B., J.C.D., The Radical Sanation of Invalid Marriages, VIII-208 pp., 1938.
117. Boffa, Rev. Conrad Humbert, J.C.D., Canonical Provisions for Catholic Schools, VII-211 pp., 1939.
118. Parsons, Rev. Anscar John, O.M.Cap., J.C.D., Canonical Elections, XII-236 pp., 1939.
119. Reilly, Rev. Edward Michael, A.B., J.C.D., The General Norms of Dispensation, XII-156 pp., 1939.
120. Ryan, Rev. Gerald Aloysius, A.B., J.C.D., Principles of Episcopal Jurisdiction, XII-172 pp., 1939.
121. Burton, Rev. Francis James, C.S.C., A.B., J.C.D., A Commentary on Canon 1125, X-222 pp., 1940.
122. Miaskiewicz, Rev. Francis Sigismund, J.C.D., Supplied Jurisdiction According to Canon 209, XII-340 pp., 1940.
123. Rice, Rev. Patrick William, A.B., J.C.D., Proof of Death in Prenuptial Investigation, VIII-156 pp., 1940.
124. Anglin, Rev. Thomas Francis, M.S., J.C.D., The Eucharistic Fast, VIII-183 pp., 1941.
125. Coleman, Rev. John Jerome, J.C.D., The Minister of Confirmation, VI-153 pp., 1941.
126. Downs, Rev. John Emmanuel, A.B., J.C.D., The Concept of Clerical Immunity, XI-163 pp., 1941.
127. Esswein, Rev. Anthony Albert, J.C.D., Extrajudicial Penal Powers of Ecclesiastical Superiors, X-144 pp., 1941.
128. Farrell, Rev. Benjamin Francis, M.A., S.T.L., J.C.D., The Rights and Duties of the Local Ordinary Regarding Congregations of Women Religious of Pontifical Approval, V-195 pp., 1941.
129. Feeney, Rev. Thomas John, A.B., S.T.L., J.C.D., Restitutio in Integrum, VI-169 pp., 1941.
130. Findlay, Rev. Stephen William, O.S.B., A.B., J.C.D., Canonical Norms Governing the Deposition and Degradation of Clerics, XVII-279 pp., 1941.

131. GOODWINE, REV. JOHN, A.B., S.T.L., J.C.D., The Right of the Church to Acquire Property, VIII-119 pp., 1941.
132. HESTON, REV. EDWARD LOUIS, C.S.C., PH.D., S.T.D., J.C.D., The Alienation of Church Property in the United States, XII-222 pp., 1941.
133. HOGAN, REV. JAMES JOHN, A.B., S.T.L., J.C.D., Judicial Advocates and Procurators, XIII-200 pp., 1941.
134. KEALY, REV. THOMAS M., A.B., LITT.B., J.C.D., Dowry of Women Religious, IX-152 pp., 1941.
135. KEENE, REV. MICHAEL JAMES, O.S.B., J.C.D., Religious Ordinaries and Canon 198, V-164 pp., 1941 (printed 1942).
136. KERIN, REV. CHARLES A., S.S., M.A., S.T.B., J.C.D., The Privation of Christian Burial, XVI-279 pp., 1941.
137. LOUIS, REV. WILLIAM FRANCIS, M.A., J.C.D., Diocesan Archives, X-101 pp., 1941.
138. MCDEVITT, REV. GILBERT JOSEPH, A.B., J.C.D., Legitimacy and Legitimation, X-247 pp., 1941.
139. MCDONOUGH, REV. THOMAS JOSEPH, A.B., J.C.D., Apostolic Administrators, X-217 pp., 1941.
140. MEIER, REV. CARL ANTHONY, A.B., J.C.D., Penal Administrative Procedure Against Negligent Pastors, XI-240 pp., 1941.
141. SCHMIDT, REV. JOHN ROGG, A.B., J.C.D., The Principles of Authentic Interpretation in Canon 17 of the Code of Canon Law, XII-331 pp., 1941.
142. SLAFKOSKY, REV. ANDREW LEONARD, A.B., J.C.D., The Canonical Episcopal Visitation of the Diocese, X-197 pp., 1941.
143. SWOBODA, REV. INNOCENT ROBERT, O.F.M., J.C.D., Ignorance in Relation to the Imputability of Delicts, IX-271 pp., 1941.
144. DUBÉ, REV. ARTHUR JOSEPH, A.B., J.C.D., The General Principles for the Reckoning of Time in Canon Law, VIII-299 pp., 1941.
145. MCBRIDE, REV. JAMES T., A.B., J.C.D., Incardination and Excardination of Seculars, XX-585 pp., 1941.
146. KRÓL, REV. JOHN T., J.C.D., The Defendant in Ecclesiastical Trials, XII-207 pp., 1942.
147. COMYNS, REV. JOSEPH J., C.SS.R., A.B., J.C.D., Papal and Episcopal Administration of Church Property, XIV-155 pp., 1942.
148. BARRY, REV. GARRETT FRANCIS, O.M.I., J.C.D., Violation of the Cloister, XII-260 pp., 1942.
149. BOLDUC, REV. GATIEN, C.S.V., A.B., S.T.L., J.C.D., Les Études dans les Religious Cléricales, VIII-155 pp., 1942.
150. BOYLE, REV. DAVID JOHN, M.A., J.C.D., The Juridic Effects of Moral Certitude on Pre-Nuptial Guarantees, XII-188 pp., 1942.
151. CANAVAN, REV. WALTER JOSEPH, M.A., LITT.D., J.C.D., The Profession of Faith, XII-143 pp., 1942.
152. DESROCHERS, REV. BRUNO, A.B., PH.L., S.T.B., J.C.D., Le Premier Concile Plénier de Québec et le Code de Droit Canonique, XIV-186 pp., 1942.

153. Dillon, Rev. Robert Edward, A.B., J.C.D., Common Law Marriage, X-148 pp., 1942.
154. Dodwell, Rev. Edward John, Ph.D., S.T.B., J.C.D., The Time and Place for the Celebration of Marriage, X-156 pp., 1942.
155. Donnellan, Rev. Thomas Andrew, A.B., J.C.D., The Obligation of the Missa pro Populo, VII-131 pp., 1942.
156. Eltz, Rev. Louis Anthony, A.B., J.C.D., Cooperation in Crime, XII-208 pp., 1942.
157. Gass, Rev. Sylvester Francis, M.A., J.C.D., Ecclesiastical Pensions, XI-206 pp., 1942.
158. Guiniven, Rev. John Joseph, C.SS.R., J.C.D., The Precept of Hearing Mass, XIV-188 pp., 1942.
159. Gulczynski, Rev. John Theophilus, J.C.D., The Desecration and Violation of Churches, X-126 pp., 1942.
160. Hammill, Rev. John Leo, M.A., J.C.D., The Obligations of the Traveler According to Canon 14, VIII-204 pp., 1942.
161. Haydt, Rev. John Joseph, A.B., J.C.D., Reserved Benefices, XI-148 pp., 1942.
162. Huser, Rev. Roger John, O.F.M., A.B., J.C.D., The Crime of Abortion in Canon Law, XII-187 pp., 1942.
163. Kearney, Rev. Francis Patrick, A.B., S.T.L., J.C.D., The Principles of Canon Law 1127, X-162 pp., 1942.
164. Linahen, Rev. Leo James, S.T.L., J.C.D., De Absolutione Complicis in Peccato Turpi, V-114 pp., 1942.
165. McCloskey, Rev. Joseph Aloysius, A.B., J.C.D., The Subject of Ecclesiastical Law According to Canon 12, XVII-246 pp., 1942 (printed 1943).
166. O'Neill, Rev. Francis Joseph, C.SS.R., J.C.D., The Dismissal of Religious in Temporary Vows, XIII-220 pp., 1942.
167. Prince, Rev. John Edward, A.B., S.T.B., J.C.D., The Diocesan Chancellor, X-136 pp., 1942.
168. Riesner, Rev. Albert Joseph, C.SS.R., J.C.D., Apostates and Fugitives from Religious Institutes, IX-168 pp., 1942.
169. Stenger, Rev. Joseph Bernard, J.C.D., The Mortgaging of Church Property, 186 pp., 1942.
170. Waldron, Rev. Joseph Francis, A.B., J.C.D., The Minister of Baptism, XII-197 pp., 1942.
171. Willett, Rev. Robert Albert, J.C.D., The Probative Value of Documents in Ecclesiastical Trials, X-124 pp., 1942.
172. Woeber, Rev. Edward Martin, M.A., J.C.D., The Interpellations, XII-161 pp., 1942.
173. Benko, Rev. Matthew Aloysius, O.S.B., M.A., J.C.D., The Abbot *Nullius,* XVI-148 pp., 1943.
174. Christ, Rev. Joseph James, M.A., S.T.L., J.C.D., Dispensation from Vindicative Penalties, XIV-285 pp., 1943.
175. Clancy, Rev. Patrick M. J., O.P., A.B., S.T.Lr., J.C.D., The Local Religious Superior, X-229 pp., 1943.

176. CLARKE, REV. THOMAS JAMES, J.C.D., Parish Societies, XII-147 pp., 1943.
177. CONNOLLY, REV. JOHN PATRICK, S.T.L., J.C.D., Synodical Examiners and Parish Priest Consultors, X-223 pp., 1943.
178. DRUMM, REV. WILLIAM MARTIN, A.B., J.C.D., Hospital Chaplains, XII-175 pp., 1943.
179. FLANAGAN, REV. BERNARD JOSEPH, A.B., S.T.L., J.C.D., The Canonical Erection of Religious Houses, X-147 pp., 1943.
180. KELLEHER, REV. STEPHEN JOSEPH, A.B., S.T.B., J.C.D., Discussions with Non-Catholics: Canonical Legislation, X-93 pp., 1943.
181. LEWIS, REV. GORDIAN, C.P., J.C.D., Chapters in Religious Institutes, XII-169 pp., 1943.
182. MARX, REV. ADOLPH, J.C.D., The Declaration of Nullity of Marriages Contracted Outside the Church, X-151 pp., 1943.
183. MATULENAS, REV. RAYMOND ANTHONY, O.S.B., A.B., J.C.D., Communication, a Source of Privileges, VII-225 pp., 1943.
184. O'LEARY, REV. CHARLES GERARD, C.SS.R., J.C.D., Religious Dismissed After Perpetual Profession, X-213 pp., 1943.
185. POWER, REV. CORNELIUS MICHAEL, J.C.D., The Blessing of Cemeteries, XII-231 pp., 1943.
186. SHUHLER, REV. RALPH VINCENT, O.S.A., J.C.D., Privileges of Religious to Absolve and Dispense, XII-195 pp., 1943.
187. ZIOLKOWSKI, REV. THADDEUS STANISLAUS, A.B., J.C.D., The Consecration and Blessing of Churches, XII-151 pp., 1943.
188. HENEGHAN, REV. JOHN JOSEPH, S.T.D., J.C.D., The Marriages of Unworthy Catholics: Canons 1065 and 1066, XVI-213 pp., 1944.
189. CARROLL, REV. COLEMAN FRANCIS, M.A., S.T.L., J.C.L., Charitable Institutions.
190. CIESLUK, REV. JOSEPH EDWARD, PH.B., S.T.L., J.C.D., National Parishes in the United States, VI-178 pp., 1944.
191. COBURN, REV. VINCENT PAUL, A.B., J.C.D., Marriages of Conscience, XII-172 pp., 1944.
192. CONNORS, REV. CHARLES PAUL, C.S.SP., A.B., J.C.D., Extra-Judicial Procurators in the Code of Canon Law, X-94 pp., 1944.
193. COYLE, REV. PAUL RAYMOND, A.B., J.C.D., Judicial Exceptions, X-142 pp., 1944.
194. FAIR, REV. BARTHOLOMEW FRANCIS, A.B., S.T.L., J.C.D., The Impediment of Abduction, XII-122 pp., 1944.
195. GALLAGHER, REV. THOMAS RAPHAEL, O.P., A.B., S.T.LR., J.C.D., The Examination of the Qualities of the Ordinand, X-166 pp., 1944.
196. GANNON, REV. JOHN MARK, S.T.L., J.C.D., The Interstices Required for the Promotion to Orders, XII-100 pp., 1944.
197. GOLDSMITH, REV. J. WILLIAM, B.C.S., S.T.L., J.C.D., The Competence of Church and State Over Marriages—Disputed Points, X-128 pp., 1944.

198. Goodwine, Rev. Joseph Gerard, A.B., S.T.B., J.C.D., The Reception of Converts, XIV-326 pp., 1944.
199. Kowalski, Rev. Romuald Eugene, O.F.M., A.B., J.C.D., Sustenance of Religious Houses of Regulars, X-174 pp., 1944.
200. McCoy, Rev. Alan Edward, O.F.M., J.C.D., Force and Fear in Relation to Delictual Imputability and Penal Responsibility, XII-160 pp., 1944.
201. McDevitt, Rev. Vincent John, Ph.B., S.T.L., J.C.L., Perjury.
202. Martin, Rev. Thomas Owen, Ph.D., S.T.D., J.C.D., Adverse Possession, Prescription and Limitation of Actions: The Canonical "Praescriptio," XX-208 pp., 1944.
203. Miklosovic, Rev. Paul John, A.B., J.C.L., Attempted Marriages and Their Consequent Juridic Effects.
204. Mundy, Rev. Thomas Maurice, A.B., S.T.L., J.C.D., The Union of Parishes, X-164 pp. 1944.
205. O'Dea, Rev. John Coyle, A.B., J.C.D., The Matrimonial Impediment of Nonage, VIII-126 pp., 1944.
206. Olalia, Rev. Alexander Ayson, S.T.L., J.C.D., A Comparative Study of the Christian Constitution of States and the Constitution of the Philippine Commonwealth, XII-136 pp., 1944.
207. Poisson, Rev. Pierre-Marie, C.S.C., A.B., Ph.L., Th.L., J.C.L., Droits Patrimoniaux des Maisons et des Eglises Religieuses.
208. Stadalnikas, Rev. Casimir Joseph, M.I.C., J.C.D., Reservation of Censures, X-141 pp., 1944.
209. Sullivan, Rev. Eugene Henry, S.T.L., J.C.D., Proof of the Reception of the Sacraments, X-165 pp., 1944.
210. Vaughan, Rev. William Edward, J.C.D., Constitutions for Diocesan Courts, X-200 pp., 1944.
211. Paro, Rev. Gino, S.T.D., J.C.D., The Right of Papal Legation, X-221 pp., 1944 (printed 1947).
212. Balzer, Rev. Ralph Francis, C.P., J.C.D., The Computation of Time in a Canonical Novitiate, X-227 pp., 1945.
213. Dougherty, Rev. John Whelan, A.B., S.T.L., J.C.D., De Inquisitione Speciali, XII-195 pp., 1945.
214. Dziob, Rev. Michael Walter, J.C.D., The Sacred Congregation for the Oriental Church, XII-181 pp., 1945.
215. Eidenschink, Rev. John Albert, O.S.B., B.A., J.C.D., The Election of Bishops in the Letters of Pope Gregory the Great, VIII-200 pp., 1945.
216. Gill, Rev. Nicholas, C.P., J.C.D., The Spiritual Prefect in Clerical Religious Houses of Study, X-140 pp., 1945.
217. Hynes, Rev. Harry Gerard, S.T.L., J.C.D., The Privileges of Cardinals, XII-183 pp., 1945.
218. McDevitt, Rev. Gerald Vincent, S.T.L., J.C.D., The Renunciation of an Ecclesiastical Office, XIV-179 pp., 1945.

219. MANNING, REV. JOSEPH LEROY, J.C.D., The Free Conferral of Offices, VII-116 pp., 1945.
220. MEYER, REV. LOUIS G., O.S.B., A.B., S.T.B., J.C.D., Alms-gathering by Religious, XII-163 pp., 1945.
221. O'DONNELL, REV. CLETUS FRANCIS, M.A., J.C.D., The Marriage of Minors, XII-268 pp., 1945.
222. PRUNSKIS, REV. JOSEPH, J.C.D., Comparative Law, Ecclesiastical and Civil, in Lithuanian Concordat, X-161 pp., 1945.
223. SWEENEY, REV. FRANCIS PATRICK, C.SS.R., J.C.D., The Reduction of Clerics to the Lay State, X-199 pp., 1945.
224. VOGELPOHL, REV. HENRY JOHN, J.C.D., The Simple Impediments to Holy Orders, XVI-190 pp., 1945.
225. BROCKHAUS, REV. THOMAS AQUINAS, O.S.B., J.C.D., Religious who are known as *Conversi*, X-127 pp., 1945.
226. GRIESE, REV. ORVILLE NICHOLAS, S.T.D., J.C.D., The Marriage Contract and the Procreation of Offspring, XVI-224 pp., 1946.
227. BOUDREAUX, REV. WARREN LOUIS, J.C.D., The *"ab acatholicis nati"* of Canon 1099, § 2, XII-110 pp., 1946.
228. BOWE, REV. THOMAS JOSEPH, A.B., J.C.D., Religious Superioresses, VIII-206 pp., 1946.
229. DIEDERICHS, REV. MICHAEL FERDINAND, S.C.J., J.C.D., The Jurisdiction of the Latin Ordinaries over their Oriental Subjects, XIV-153 pp., 1946.
230. DINGMAN, REV. MAURICE JOHN, A.B., S.T.L., J.C.L., The Plaintiff in Contentious Trials.
231. FRISON, REV. BASIL, C.M.F., M.MUS., J.C.D., The Retroactivity of Law, X-221 pp., 1946.
232. CALVIN, REV. WILLIAM ANTHONY, M.A., J.C.D., The Administrative Transfer of Pastors, XII-288 pp., 1946.
233. GORACY, REV. JOSEPH C., J.C.L., The Diriment Matrimonial Impediment of Major Orders.
234. HALE, REV. JOSEPH FRANCIS, M.A., S.T.L., J.C.D., The Pastor of Burial, X-247 pp., 1946 (printed 1949).
235. HENRY, REV. JOSEPH ARTHUR, A.B., J.C.D., The Mass and Holy Communion: Interritual Law, XII-138 pp., 1946.
236. LINENBERGER, REV. HERBERT, C.PP.S., J.C.D., The False Denunciation of an Innocent Confessor, VIII-205 pp., 1946 (1949).
237. LOWRY, REV. JAMES MARTIN, A.B., J.C.D., Dispensation from Private Vows, XII-266 pp., 1946.
238. LYNCH, REV. GEORGE EDWARD, A.B., S.T.L., J.C.D., Coadjutors and Auxiliaries of Bishops, X-107 pp., 1946 (printed 1947).
239. LYNCH, REV. TIMOTHY, M.S.SS.T., J.C.D., Contracts between Bishops and Religious Congregations, XIII-232 pp., 1946.
240. McCLUNN, REV. JUSTIN DAVID, A.B., S.T.L., J.C.D., Administrative Recourse, VII-142 pp., 1946.

241. LOHMULLER, REV. MARTIN NICHOLAS, A.B., J.C.D., The Promulgation of Law, XII-140 pp., 1947.
242. MCGRATH, REV. JAMES, A.B., J.C.D., The Privilege of the Canon, XII-156 pp., 1946.
243. MARBACH, REV. JOSEPH FRANCIS, A.B., J.C.D., Marriage Legislation for the Catholics of the Oriental Rites in the United States and Canada, XIV-314 pp., 1946.
244. SHIMKUS, REV. BERNARD ALOYSIUS, A.B., J.C.L., The Determination and Transfer of Rite.
245. SMITH, REV. VINCENT MICHAEL, A.B., S.T.L., J.C.L., Ignorance Affecting Matrimonial Consent.
246. WACHTRLE, REV. PAUL ANTHONY, A.B., J.C.L., The Baptism of the Children of Non-Catholics.
247. CROTTY, REV. MATTHEW MICHAEL, J.C.D., The Recipient of First Holy Communion, X-142 pp., 1947.
248. EAGLETON, REV. GEORGE, J.C.D., The Quinquennial Faculties, Formula IV, XIV-199 pp., 1947 (printed 1948).
249. GIBBONS, REV. MARION LEO, C.M., J.C.L., Domicile of the Wife Unlawfully Separated from Her Husband, XIV-171 pp., 1947.
250. KELLY, REV. BERNARD M., S.T.L., J.C.D., The Functions Reserved to Pastors, XII-141 pp., 1947.
251. KILCULLEN, REV. THOMAS J., LL.M., J.C.D., The Collegiate Moral Person as Party Litigant, X-150 pp., 1947.
252. LAFONTAINE, REV. GERMAINE JOSEPH, W.F., J.C.D., Relations Canoniques entre le Missionaire et Ses Superieurs, X-117 pp., 1947.
253. LANE, REV. LORAS THOMAS, A.B., S.T.L., J.C.D., Matrimonial Procedure in the Ordinary Court of Second Instance, XVI-184 pp., 1947.
254. LOVER, REV. JAMES FRANCIS, C.Ss.R., J.C.D., The Master of Novices, X-168 pp., 1947.
255. MCNICHOLAS, REV. TIMOTHY JOSEPH, J.C.D., The *Septimae Manus* Witness, XII-133 pp., 1947 (printed 1949).
256. MAROSITZ, REV. JOSEPH JOHN, M.S.C., J.C.D., Obligations and Privileges of Religious Promoted to the Episcopal or Cardinalitial Dignities, XII-180 pp., 1947.
257. MURPHY, REV. FRANCIS JOSEPH, J.C.D., Legislative Powers of the Provincial Council, XII-158 pp., 1947.
258. O'BRIEN, REV. ROMAEUS WILLIAM, O.CARM., J.C.D., The Provincial Superior in Religious Orders of Men, X-294 pp., 1947.
259. PFALLER, REV. BENEDICT ANTHONY, O.S.B., J.C.D., *The ipso facto* Effected Dismissal of Religious, XII-225 pp., 1947.
260. POPEK, REV. ALPHONSE SYLVESTER, J.C.D., The Rights and Obligations of Metropolitans, XX-460 pp., 1947.
261. RISTUCCIA, REV. BERNARD JOSEPH, C.M., J.C.D., Quasi-Religious, XVI-318 pp., 1947 (printed 1949).
262. SONNTAG, REV. NATHANIEL LOUIS, O.F.M.CAP., J.C.D., Censorship of Special Classes of Books, XII-147 pp., 1947.

263. Stadler, Rev. Joseph Nicholas, J.C.D., Frequent Holy Communion, X-158 pp., 1947.
264. Szal, Rev. Ignatius Joseph, J.C.D., The Communication of Catholics with Schismatics, XII-217 pp., 1947.
265. Wagner, Rev. Urban S., O.F.M., Conv., J.C.D., Parochial Substitute Vicars and Supplying Priests, IX-126 pp., 1947.
266. Quinn, Rev. Joseph, M.A., J.C.D., Documents Required for the Reception of Orders, XIV-207 pp., 1948.
267. Bennington, Rev. James Clement, A.B., J.C.L., The Recipient of Confirmation.
268. Blaher, Rev. Damian Joseph, O.F.M., A.B., J.C.D., The Ordinary Processes in Causes of Beatification and Canonization, XVI-290 pp., 1948 (printed 1949).
269. Clune, Rev. Robert Bell, B.A., J.C.D., The Judicial Interrogation of the Parties, XII-142 pp., 1948.
270. Courtemanche, Rev. Basil F., B.A., J.C.D., The Total Simulation of Matrimonial Consent, XX-120 pp., 1948.
271. Dlouhy, Rev. Maur John, O.S.B., A.B., J.C.L., The Ordination of Exempt Religious.
272. Donovan, Rev. John Thomas, Ph.B., S.T.L., J.C.D., The Clerical Obligation of Canons 138 and 140, XII-209 pp., 1948.
273. Freking, Rev. Frederick W., A.B., S.T.B., J.C.D., The Canonical Installation of Pastors, XII-210 pp., 1948.
274. Fulton, Rev. Thomas B., J.C.D., Prenuptial Investigation, XII-190 pp., 1948.
275. Godley, Rev. James P., J.C.D., Time and Place for the Celebration of Mass, X-206 pp., 1948 (printed 1949).
276. Kane, Rev. Thomas A., A.B., B.S., J.C.D., Jurisdiction of the Patriarchs of the Major Sees in Antiquity and in the Middle Ages, XII-111 pp., 1948 (printed 1949).
277. Kennedy, Rev. Andrew A., J.C.L., The Annual Pastoral Report to the Local Ordinary.
278. Konrad, Rev. Joseph George, J.C.D., Transfer of Religious to Another Community, VIII-284 pp., 1948 (printed 1949).
279. Kress, Rev. Alphonse, J.C.L., Contumacy in Ecclesiastical Trials.
280. McCartney, Rev. Marcellus Anthony, O.F.M., M.A., J.C.D., Faculties of Regular Confessors, XII-164 pp., 1948 (printed 1949).
281. McCaslin, Rev. Edward Patrick, M.A., S.T.L., J.C.L., The Division of Parishes.
282. McElroy, Rev. Francis J., A.B., J.C.L., The Privileges of Bishops.
283. Quinn, Rev. Stephen, M.S.SS.T., J.C.D., Relation Between the Local Ordinary and Religious of Diocesan Approval, XII-153 pp., 1948 (printed 1949).
284. Schneider, Rev. Edelhard Louis, S.D.S., B.A., J.C.L., The Status of Secularized Ex-Religious Clerics, X-155 pp., 1948.

285. Thompson, Chester J., A.B., J.C.L., The Simple Removal from Office.
286. O'Brien, Rev. Kenneth R., A.B., J.C.D., The Nature of Support of Diocesan Priests in the United States, XVI-162 pp., 1949.
287. Metz, Rev. John E., S.T.L., J.C.D., The Recording Judge in the Ecclesiastical Collegiate Tribunal, X-130 pp., 1949.
288. Reinhardt, Rev. Marion J., S.T.L., J.C.D., The Rogatory Commission, XIII-182 pp., 1949.
289. Ortega Uhiuk, Rev. Juan, S.J., J.C.L., De Delicto Sollicitationis.
290. Casey, Rev. James V., J.C.D., A Study of Canon 2222 § 1, XII-127 pp., 1949.
291. Allgeier, Rev. Joseph L., J.C.D., The Canonical Obligation of Preaching in Parish Churches, X-115 pp., 1949 (printed 1950).
292. Cahill, Rev. Daniel R., J.C.D., The Custody of the Holy Eucharist, XVI-178 pp., 1949 (printed 1950).
293. Carr, Rev. Aiden, O.F.M., Carm., S.T.D., J.C.L., Vocation to the Priesthood: Its Canonical Concept.
294. Knopke, Rev. Roch F., O.F.M., J.C.D., Reverential Fear in Matrimonial Cases in Asiatic Countries: Rota Cases, XII-112 pp., 1949.
295. Lavelle, Rev. Howard D., J.C.D., The Obligation of Holding Sacred Missions in Parishes, XVI-142 pp., 1949.
296. Mickells, Rev. Anthony B., J.C.L., The Constitutive Elements of Parishes.
297. Noone, Rev. John J., J.C.D., Nullity in Judicial Acts, X-147 pp., 1949 (printed 1950).
298. Sheehan, Rev. Daniel E., J.C.L., The Minister of Holy Communion.
299. Statkus, Rev. Francis J., J.C.L., The Minister of the Last Sacraments.
300. Cook, Rev. John P., J.C.D., Ecclesiastical Communities and Their Ability to Induce Legal Customs, XII-152 pp., 1949 (printed 1950).
301. Fazzalaro, Rev. Francis J., J.C.D., The Place for the Hearing of Confessions, X-150 pp., 1949 (printed 1950).
302. Hannan, Rev. Philip M., J.C.D., The Canonical Concept of *congrua sustentatio* for the Secular Clergy, XII-237 pp., 1949 (printed 1950).
303. Quinn, Rev. Hugh G., S.T.L., J.C.L., The Particular Penal Precept.
304. Gallagher, Rev. John F., J.C.L., The Matrimonial Impediment of Public Propriety.
305. Welsh, Rev. Thomas J., J.C.L., The Use of the Portable Altar.
306. Waters, Rev. Joseph L., S.S.J., J.C.L., The Probation in Societies of Quasi-Religious.
307. Regan, Rev. Michael J., J.C.L., Canon 16.
308. Byrne, Rev. Harry J., J.C.L., Investment of Church Funds.
309. Gallagher, Rev. Thomas V., J.C.L., The Rejection of Judicial Witnesses and Testimony.
310. Chatham, Rev. Josiah G., Ph.B., S.T.L., J.C.L., Force and Fear as Invalidating Marriage: the Element of Injustice, XIV-183 pp., 1950.
311. Brown, Rev. James Victor, O.R.S.A., J.C.L., The Invalidating Effects of Force, Fear, and Fraud Upon the Canonical Novitiate.

312. Duerr, Rev. Charles J., B.A., J.C.L., The Judicial Notary.
313. Gonzalez, Rev. Francisco J., O.S.A., J.C.L., De Parocho Religioso Eiusque Superiore Locali.
314. Hannon, Rev. James J., J.C.L., Holy Viaticum.
315. Sadlowski, Rev. Erwin L., J.C.L., The Sacred Furnishings of Churches.
316. Sego, Rev. Arthur A., J.C.L., Dispensation From the Interpellations.
317. Waterhouse, Rev. John M., J.C.L., The Power of the Local Ordinary to Impose a Matrimonial Ban.
318. Frein, Rev. Eugene B., J.C.L., The Discretionary Power of the Defender of the Matrimonial Bond.
319. Carton, Rev. George A., J.C.L., The Time Factor in the Gaining of Indulgences.
320. Walsh, Rev. John J., C.S.Sp., J.C.L., The Jurisdiction of the Inter-ritual Confessor in the United States and Canada.
321. Unterkoefler, Rev. Ernest L., S.T.L., J.C.L., The Presiding Judge in Matrimonial Causes of First Instance.

www.ingramcontent.com/pod-product-compliance
Lightning Source LLC
LaVergne TN
LVHW050217080826
844660LV00012B/425
9780813224619